julia bradbury's

RAILWAY WALKS

I would like to bestow my enormous thanks to
the team for their creative spirit and tremendous
support. In particular thank you Eric Harwood for your
friendship, editorial guidance and for being a top man
in telly. Clare Jones for your interpretation of the stories
and the landscape, alongside your calming influence and
happy demeanour, and Gina my cornerstone and sister;
I couldn't walk a step without you. The programmes are
not possible without the whole crew – thank you all for
making the magic come to life. My gratitude to Richard
Klein at the BBC for his continued sustentation, without
whom none of this would have happened. Finally Mum
and Dad, Chrissi and Michael – thank you.

Frances Lincoln Ltd
4 Torriano Mews
Torriano Avenue
London NW5 2RZ
www.franceslincoln.com

British Library Cataloguing in Publication Data
A catalogue record for this book is available from
the British Library.

ISBN: 9780711231672

Printed and bound in Slovenia

9 8 7 6 5 4 3 2 1

Opposite: Penmaenpool Toll Bridge across the Mawddach Estuary, Wales.
Previous page: Looking south down Loch Lubnaig in Callander.

CONTENTS

*Opposite: View looking south down
Glen Ogle with Glen Ogle Viaduct
to the right.*

You know what happens; you're waiting at the platform for ages, you give up hope, buy a hot drink and then your train pulls in. You can't get on because it's impossible to manage your luggage and the boiling hot refreshment without scorching yourself or the young child next to you.

Trains. Don't you just luv 'em? Since I filmed the Railways Walks series for the BBC I've become an unlikely figurehead for the railway networks and trains, and everybody assumes I do love them. Now when I travel by train I am met with knowing glances and often the conductor will engage in a little 'train chat'. I have been asked to get involved in an awful lot of train stuff and to pen the odd choo choo piece. Don't get me wrong. I'm not complaining and nor do I want you to think I took the money and boarded coach H not giving a tosh. I love travelling by train. My Dad is a steam locomotive enthusiast so I grew up visiting Peak Rail as a nipper. Trains were a big birthday present theme of his for an unhealthy stretch of time so my family and I have engaged with a lot of train paraphernalia over the years. But I would categorically like to declare here and now that I am not a train nerd, or buff, or over-enthusiast. I simply like them, have become increasingly interested in the history of our lost railway empire and quite like the tea on the First Great Western from Newport to London Paddington, which is what I'm on now as I write this. The resulting train related enquiries have been many and varied since Railway Walks was screened and lots of people have asked about 'a book to go with the series'. So here it is. They're lovely walks and worthy of compilation in this book.

When I was the apple of my father's eye we would explore the Peak District together. He was born in Tideswell, Derbyshire and so as a child I was taken to his patch and was captivated by its beauty. I must admit that the history of the place wasn't what enthralled me back then – the railways, the mining, the elegant country estates all just looked nice. But then I got older and the colourful, painful and inspiring story of the railway

Julia at Glenoglehead Loch

industry and its decline began to intrigue me. In 1913 Britain's railway empire was booming. An intricate web of networks and lines serviced the country with more than 23,000 miles of track. But after World War One competition came from buses, cars and even air travel. After World War Two came nationalisation, and not too long after that Dr Beeching wielded his axe. Thousands of miles of track and thousands of stations were closed. Hordes of people lost their jobs. Communities were cut off, industries collapsed. Why reinvest when a big chop would do? That was Beeching's ideology. A closure protest movement was born – the Railway Development Association – but even with the influential poet John Betjeman on board it made little impact (although he did manage to help save the glorious St Pancras Station, which was also under threat – thank the train gods in the sky). So now we are left with the remnants, which amount to about 9,000 or 10,000 miles or so of disused lines, a hushed world of embankments, redundant platforms and viaducts – prime walking turf.

Geographically these railway walks cover a good cross section of the country from Scotland in the north down to Weymouth on the south coast. Every walk is in such a prime setting that you could easily build a weekend break around each one with plenty to take in other than the hike itself. Of course it helps to have your luggage with you. Sadly I didn't have mine when I started the Cornish walk at Portreath Harbour. I came straight from another location but my bag didn't. The filming schedule for the series is quite tight so what we couldn't afford to do was to wait for my bag to arrive. This meant Annabel our production assistant had to donate her trousers to the cause. Now a lot of people ask me about my trousers – men and women. Men want to buy them for their wives or girlfriends and women want to know where they're from because they have unusual embroidery detail on them. Annabel's troos are devoid of said embroidery and that Dear Reader is why of all the walks I have filmed I am sporting 'naked trousers' on the Portreath to Devoran trail. (I am sorry to include this trivial detail but you have no idea how many people ask about exactly this type of thing!)

The Monsal Trail in and around the peaks of Derbyshire is one of my favourites of course. Roughly eight miles from Bakewell to Blackwell Mill, the walk owes its existence to the Midland Railway that ran from London to Manchester, cutting through the heart of the Peaks. People love steam trains and this is one of the rare spots in the country where you can see how the Victorians did it 140 years ago on the Peak Rail service between Matlock and Darley Dale, which 40,000 people visit each year. When the Midland Railway was first proposed the engineers must have thrown down their chamfer cutters in despair. Carving through the limestone hills of the Wye Valley was surely impossible? But six tunnels are proof that they managed. The giant Headstone Tunnel bursts out 80 feet above the River Wye on to the famous five-arched viaduct – surely one of the most beautiful in all England. Can you imagine what it must have been like for the Victorians glancing out of the window as the train exploded into daylight? What an extraordinary view. I enjoyed the section of the walk following the line towards Great Longstone Station which is right next to the Thornbridge Estate. What you notice as you pass the old station is how real it feels – and of course it is real – but you actually expect to hear a train parping up the rear at any moment. You also notice a rather ornate building right next door to the station. It was the brainchild of former resident of Thornbridge Hall George Marples – a portly silver moustached business man from Sheffield who decided in 1896 to build his own private terminal right next to the original. He had a bit of a reputation as a ladies man, and who can resist a squire with his very own platform? For me this area holds a sentimental place in my heart. I can imagine my Dad and his younger brother capering around the hills doing what young boys did in the 1950s. Dad recently took his grandson Jack back to the stream

*Julia overlooking Penmaenpool Toll Bridge
across the Mawddach Estuary, Wales.*

INTRODUCTION

where he taught me to tickle trout found resting under a watery ledge. The stream is no more. Like the forgotten railway line the riverbed lies dried up, the displaced fishy communities swimming somewhere else.

The two Scottish walks included in this series filled me with great joy and got me into a spot of trouble. Firstly I would like to apologise again for my mispronunciation of a few words and places. Of course we thought we had it right, and asked locals' advice but in the speed of filming, with a group of Brits for counsel on the day it wasn't perfect. (I'm Welsh-Greek, so no help at all.) I had a particularly disgruntled email from Mr Sandy McGill, 64, telling me that having taken his life in his hands by telling Mrs McGill that he had installed me as his 'new heart throb', he all but changed his mind after two episodes full of a 'plethora of mispronunciations'. I was able to mollify him, but had to promise to practice pronouncing 'loch' as in 'Bach' and not as in 'lock'.

In Aberlour I got to do something that I have never been allowed to do before or since in a televised walk. I had a drink … or two. And the reason for my foray into alcohol, well it was all part of the story, of course. Good investigation and research I thought. The Mash Tun is the unmistakable public house, conveniently positioned just off the walking route and easily found right next to the old wooden slatted Aberlour Station, which is now a Speyside Way information centre. In terms of whisky production its name refers to the vessel used to mix the three key ingredients – water, malted barley and yeast. The landlord Mark Braidwood poured me a selection of fine drams and I settled down to learn a thing or two about the true etiquette of whisky consumption … that it should be taken at room temperature, and that whisky oxidises in the bottle so you should always order from a nearly full bottle. This was important research but I understand you may well feel the need to check up on my facts yourself. After my taste of the very peaty local 'Aberlour' itself (my fourth in half an hour) I was very happy – a full smile stretched across my mush, conveying my proletarian

appreciation. I definitely don't have much of a whisky nose – and there is no way in my mind you can combine whisky drinking with walking. Not even a wee dram. It was a bit wibbly wobbly for the next few miles.

Walking is one of the few activities that cut accross age, profession, social demographics and sex. You can be a springy seven year old or a sprightly septuagenarian and enjoy walking. There is nothing more therapeutic than roaming across great expanses of wild wonderful countryside or taking in the atmosphere and architecture on an urban stroll. Millions of people hit the hills and the streets every week and you don't need to be an athlete to engage in the most popular sport in the land. I get letters from six year olds and eighty year olds alike who enjoy and participate in perambulation. And that I think is why railway walks are so appealing. Hills, mountains, Munros and fells can seem threatening and challenging. A pleasant stroll along a level railway line can be more comforting and a little easier on the limbs. As the American poet David McCord said 'A pedestrian is a man in danger of his life. A walker is a man in possession of his soul'. I wish you a most enjoyable journey.

the birth of steam

For a number of reasons this railway walk promises to be quite an adventure. For a start you will be walking right across the country, from the north Cornish coast to its counterpart in the south. There'll also be not one, but two railway lines, the Portreath Tramroad and the Redruth and Chasewater line, both of which date back further than any of the other railway explorations in this book. Today, these lines are conveniently linked and waymarked by Cornwall's Coast to Coast Trail. It might also come as a surprise to learn that the world's first steam locomotive was built by a Cornishman. But Richard Trevithick's greatest contribution to his home county was the building of high-pressure steam engines for local mines. So this really does promise to be a journey into the complex history of Cornish mining and one which truly heralds the birth of the steam age.

One of the many engine houses that remain in Cornwall.

CORNWALL

history of the railway line

The Portreath Tramroad forged a route from the north Cornish coast deep into copper and tin mining territory. Work on laying the track began in Portreath in 1809 and the complete six mile track to Crofthandy was in use by 1819, directly connecting Portreath harbour with the mines at North Downs and Poldice. The Bassets of Tehidy, the Foxes of Falmouth and the Williams of Scorrier built and owned the tramroad, until then most of minerals had been transported over unmade roads by trains of horses with panniers.

The need for an integrated transport system combining a rail link and a harbour became increasingly apparent. Smelting copper, as opposed to tin, required much more coal and it was more economical to send the copper to the nearest coalfields. From Portreath these were in south Wales. But the power hungry machines of the copper and tin mining industries also required enormous quantities of coal. So by the 1840s Portreath was well used by the 'Welsh Fleet' taking copper ore to Wales and bringing engine coal back.

Despite this mutually beneficial flow of goods, by the late 1860s copper production was slumping and Portreath then relied simply on coal traffic for business, although timber and other mining materials were also imported. Following the depression of the 1920s and growing competition from rail and road transport, the port had all but ceased to trade by the early 1930s. The line officially closed on New Year's Day 1936. The rails were however not lifted until 1945 and for the duration of World War Two the line was used for storing wagons in case the nearby storage yards were bombed. The

Aerial view of the walk crossing under the Carnon Viaduct which carries the still active trainline to Falmouth.

tracks were kept as a possible supply route to RAF Portreath, then an important airfield.

The second line of the walk, the Redruth & Chasewater Railway was the creation of John Taylor, controller of the massive Consolidated Mines. Taylor's business was so large that it warranted the building of a new railway, which opened in 1824 and carried 50,000 tonnes of ore in its first year. But Taylor's railway also started to go into decline, another victim of the global slump in copper prices. The Redruth & Chasewater Railway eventually ground to a complete halt in 1918.

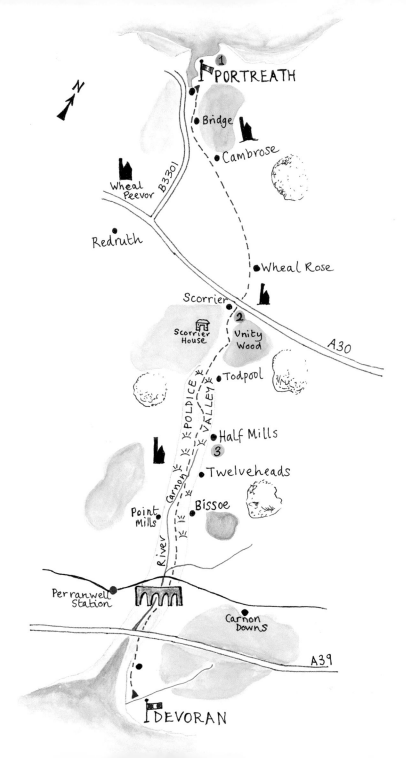

THE WALK
Portreath to The Point, Devoran
12 miles / 19.3 kilometres

OVERVIEW

You head east from Portreath harbour on a footpath above
Bridge, before the route curves through Cambrose. The walk
then continues through an area of farmland in an easterly and
then southeasterly direction reaching the villages of Wheal
Rose and Scorrier. There's then a winding detour through
Unity Wood before entering the heart of mining country,
passing old industrial communities like Todpool and the
unmistakable Poldice Valley. This was the end of the line
for the Portreath Tramroad. But as you head towards the
south coast, you pick up the second railway, the Redruth &
Chasewater, which followed the valley of the Carnon River
and passed underneath the viaduct of today's active rail line
to Falmouth. The village of Devoran, sitting at the top of a
long estuary, is the first sign of the end of the walk. But you
follow the water's edge all the way to the mooring point at the
old railway terminus.

STAGE 1

Portreath to Wheal Peevor

Portreath Harbour.

The walk starts at the dramatic entrance to Portreath harbour. With all its rocks and cliffs this has always been a notoriously difficult harbour for ships to enter, which is why it might seem all the more surprising that in 1820 it was described as Cornwall's most important port. But as this walk is about to reveal, the harbour had a key role to play in the development of the nearby mining industries.

Unlike many of my railway walks there's no station to start from. The reason for that is quite simple, this line didn't carry passengers. It was in fact, a tramroad, a kind of forerunner of the modern railway formed of track, sleepers and signals. This track was designed purely to transport materials to and from the mines. They generally had a far more industrial purpose and were usually linked to mines, factories or quarries and were used to move materials around via horse-drawn trams or wagons. At least some of the tracks of the Portreath Tramroad were made from blocks of stone judging by the few granite sets that still remain.

The walk starts on the eastern side of Portreath harbour. This is where the tramroad started from and today it's where Cornwall's Coast to Coast Trail begins. The harbour owes its very existence to the development of local copper mining in the 1700s because it was used to ship the copper for smelting to the nearest coalfields in south Wales. One local family in particular played a leading role in funding the harbour's construction and so for many years it was known simply as Basset's Cove (a name that will crop up again on the walk).

The route of the tramroad was a key feature of this seaside village but a hundred and fifty years has been more

Aerial view of Basset monument, Carn Brea.

than enough time to obscure its route entirely and so this walk starts with a stroll through the backstreets of Portreath. The walk is signposted for the Coast to Coast Trail and it leaves the harbour heading inland between shops and past the Porteath Arms Pub before following Sunnyvale Road east out of Portreath.

After forking left onto a footpath the route leaves the modern tarmac behind and begins to take on a more expected feel up a gentle incline. This isn't a walk where you'll immediately find overgrown platforms and crumbling locomotive sheds. The remains of Cornwall's first railway are subtle to say the least. But they're there if you look out for them. If you look carefully you will find original granite sets that the tramroad used to run on, sort of like early railway sleepers.

As you continue on the footpath keep an eye out to your right and you should be able to spot the outskirts of Redruth, once the main mining town in the area. The thimble of a monument, just beyond and to your right, was built using donations from a grateful public to honour local mine owner Baron Basset.

Julia walking along the tramroad before reaching Cambrose.

In his time, the Baron helped build defences around Plymouth and campaigned against slavery. He also left behind him the bustling town of Redruth, a place that exploded into prominence once the neighbouring seams of tin and copper had been found.

Soon, you will see your first glimpse of some mine engine houses. Just ahead is a clearing with a convenient place to sit. From here you will glimpse three chimney stacks on the horizon. This is Wheal Peevor, reputably the best preserved engine house in the area.

Engine houses are very much a symbol of this part of Cornwall and the remains of over two hundred are still left intact today. These fields were once littered with industrial chimneys and there would have been hundreds more. Many were dismantled and rebuilt elsewhere as mines opened and closed.

Wheal Peevor

Wheal Peevor is actually off the main route although a brief diversion can be made. The grace and stature of the engine houses is striking, particularly set on such a hill top as here and it's a great spot to understand some of the industrial history, which has shaped so much of this walk.

When you stand looking at these ruins it's almost hard to believe that a hundred years ago this was one of the wealthiest places in Britain. That wealth owes much to the man who is known affectionately in these parts as 'Captain Dick'.

Richard Trevithick is clearly something of a local hero, a phenomenal engineer and the inventor of the high-pressure steam engine. Born just over four miles away in the village of Tregajorran, between Cambourne and nearby Redruth, he was the son of a mine captain. As a child he spent many an hour studying the steam engines as they pumped water from the deep tin and copper mines.

This fascination led to his later, great discovery. He realized that improvements in boiler technology allowed high-pressure steam or 'strong steam' to be produced safely. This meant that engines no longer relied on a condensing process and so could be smaller, lighter and run more efficiently.

But Trevithick wasn't just vital to the success of Cornwall's mining industry, in 1801 he built the 'Puffing Devil', the world's first self propelled road vehicle. Its first outing was on Christmas Eve and it successfully carried several men up Cambourne Hill, the first effective demonstration of transportation by steam. By 1804 he moved on to produce the world's first railway engine. So far from being a sleepy rural backwater, Cornwall was in fact vital to the birth of the railway age because this is where the use of the steam engine really took off in the mines. It was a revolution, which helped turn Trevithick's attention to the other uses of steam, paving the way for steam locomotion and the railway as we know it…now that's a pretty impressive legacy.

Aerial view of Wheal Peevor.

Wheal Peevor is a rare example of a three engine house arrangement. The three buildings consist of a pumping engine house, to pump water out of the mine; the winding engine house, to hoist ore and waste rock; and the stamps engine house, the engine which powered the ore crushing machines (called stamps). Noise from the stamps, which worked 24 hours could be heard almost three miles away so it must have been pretty deafening for workers up close.

'Wheal' is Cornish for a mine and 'Peevor' may have been the name of one of the mine's mineral lords or investors. The mining game was all about speculation and back in the old days when you dug a hole you didn't always know what you were going to find. And that was exactly the case at Wheal Peevor. In the mid 1700s it started as a copper mine but as the digging got deeper, it was tin that took over, reaching a peak in 1880, the era when the present pumping house and mine shaft were in full operation.

From Wheal Peevor you get a great view of the walk so far, back down the valley to Portreath and the north coast. You can see how much higher this spot is than Portreath and how much the tramroad had to climb to get here.

STAGE 2

Scorrier to Poldice

Aerial view of Scorrier House.

If you look at the map there are 'wheals' all over the place. There's Wheal Rose, Wheal Plenty and Wheal Busy. Back on the tramroad the industrial communities come thick and fast as you head southeast to Wheal Rose.

But things didn't stand still for long, by 1819, the line was extended further inland from here, right through the estate of John Williams, a mine owner, shipping and smelting magnate and a chief investor in the Portreath Tramroad.

Scorrier House is still owned by Williams' descendants and remains a private estate, which means temporarily leaving the track bed behind. Instead this walk continues by heading across the A30 and through Scorrier, past the Fox and Hounds Pub, and along the B3298. The standard Coast to Coast Trail continues, but you can take a brief and slightly more scenic diversion by taking a left hand path into Unity Wood, an ancient forest recorded in the Doomsday book. Cornwall's Coast to Coast Trail has developed around the spines of the two main mining railways and even here in the depths of Unity Wood you're only ever metres away from industrial heritage and the buildings of the eighteenth and nineteenth century tin mines can soon be spotted.

It's certainly a walk of contrasts, but the wood doesn't last for long before yet another change of scene. The collection of mining cottages at Todpool is a very quiet place today, but this was once a village that sat precariously on the edge of the vast and varied operations of the Poldice Valley.

As you head east you enter the Poldice Valley, which does a good impression of looking something like a lunar surface. It might be quiet today but two hundred years ago over fifty thousand people worked the mines here, so great were the

Building ruins in Poldice Valley.

tin prospects. In fact, since medieval times this landscape has been carved up to produce tin, copper and Cornwall's less heralded resource of arsenic. As you continue down the valley a hotch-potch world of mining detritus still harbours white piles of dust, known simply as 'The Sands', the barren remains of the arsenic works that operated till 1929.

The presence of arsenic was first discovered when the miners, who often worked up to their waists in water, realized the water was very acidic. Initially this was problematic because it meant you didn't get pure tin but the miners soon realised that by roasting it out, it could be used as a pesticide. So far from being a nuisance it became another product from the mine and was exported across the world. In Scandinavia it was used to clarify glass and as an ingredient for sheep dips in Australia and New Zealand. It was also used as a poison, in soap for cleaning leather and to produce the green pigments loved by the Victorians. The industry revived in

Aerial view of Poldice Valley.

both world wars because arsenic was needed in poison gas. But when you look around today you'll see there are barren pieces of land which still haven't recovered from the arsenic poisoning in the ground.

After walking a mile or so down the Poldice Valley the second railway line of the walk makes its first appearance, as the Redruth & Chasewater line coming from Redruth merges with the footpath. You are now firmly back on trackbed.

The Redruth and Chasewater Railway managed to achieve something that the Portreath Tramroad never did and that was to swap horse-drawn carriages for steam engines. In 1854, they introduced two; one was called Miner, the other Smelter. A third engine called Spitfire joined the line in 1859.

STAGE 3

Hale Mills to Devoran

Aerial view towards Devoran.

Before the miners had worked out a way to pump water out of the mineshafts, they used to drain it in nearby reservoirs and the flat area, which now dominates the walk, was one of the beds of such a reservoir. It's called Bissa Pool but as you can see there's no longer a pool at all.

You then pass through Hale Mills, with its collection of reed beds, which helped deal with the pollution from the mines. This remarkable passage through Poldice leads to the village of Twelveheads on your left. Now, I'm told the village is supposedly named after the large number of stamping heads that the local crushing engine possessed but there's no sign of such an engine today to check whether that could be true or not. One other local legend has left his mark though.

The Methodist Church and the Old School House in Twelveheads were the work of one Billy Bray, a miner born in the village in 1794 who witnessed the building of both railway lines serving the valley. He described himself as "drunken and lascivious" in his youth but he turned himself around to become a celebrated preacher and evangelist, noted for his good influence on his fellow miners throughout the area. The mine owners must have loved him.

Much like the railway itself, the last part of my walk follows the Carnon River towards the all-important coastline at Devoran, crossing underneath the still active line which connects Plymouth with Falmouth. Running east west, this had to span a wide valley, a challenge that was handed to none other than Isambard Kingdom Brunel.

It seems that poor Brunel didn't have quite enough budget to do his job properly and so to save money he used timber fans to prop up the tracks. But as he predicted just seventy years later, the entire viaduct had to be replaced; not up to his usual standards at all.

As you walk southeast under this still active railway viaduct you can see both the original and the replacement. When work started on Brunel's viaduct builders found they

Marker stone at Old Carnon Bridge.

had to dig through thirty feet of silt and mining spoils to reach the solid floor of the valley.

You continue along the river as it widens and opens up. The end of the walk is soon in sight as the south coast comes into view. Devoran used to be a major port, a busy interchange between the steam locomotives and the waiting boats in the estuary's deep waters. The village hall today is actually the old maintenance shed for the likes of Miner and Smelter, because this is as far as the locomotives went. The end of the walk, much like the beginning, is along a simple tramroad. An extra mile used to transfer coal and metal ore to ships further down the estuary.

Head down towards the quayside and you have reached the final chapter on this railway walk. In 1900, this was where the railway ended, a quayside known simply as Point, a classic Cornish beauty spot but the end to a very industrial walk.

But even this picture perfect Cornish estuary couldn't escape the presence of the mining industry. Just around the corner from the quayside there was a tin smelting works and long before that, even before the railway, teams would have been working in the estuary sifting through the sand and gravel looking for scraps of tin ore. This really was a world devoted to extracting as much from the ground as possible.

Julia at the end of the walk at Point, Devoran.

This is a fascinating walk through a varied and often manmade landscape, but most of all it's a walk which takes you through the changing fortunes of a vast local industry. And let's not forget, this is where the steam engine first showed its true potential, something that all the other railway walks can be very grateful for.

Additional Information:

START OF WALK: Redruth is the nearest train station to the start of the walk. Bus services then provide a link to Portreath.

END OF WALK: Perranwell is the nearest train station to Devoran (on the Plymouth/Falmouth line) and is about 1.5 miles from the main town centre. A bus service links back to Portreath via Truro.

First Devon & Cornwall are the largest bus operator in Cornwall, and operate many of the local and longer distance services. Contact: 01752 402060.

Hopley's Coaches run a small number of services. For details of their services call 01872 553786.

Recommended Maps: Redruth & St. Agnes, 104 OS Explorer

the peak express

Almost 140 years ago Victorian rail engineers were set the unlikely task of creating a mainline between London and Manchester that could negotiate the twisting valleys and rocky hills of the Peak District. Today, that same route is a favourite for walkers, cyclists and those seeking to escape the surrounding hubbub of the Midlands. This walk follows the former railway line through the Peaks, from Bakewell, almost as far as the spa town of Buxton. It's a walk that quite literally cuts right through the heart of the Peaks, through its geology, through its history as well as through its landscape.

Disused viaduct at Miller's Dale.

history of the railway line

This popular walk owes its existence to the Midland Railway. In 1867 they completed their mainline from London to Manchester, which allowed express trains to travel through the heart of the Peak District. It was a key development, providing direct access to St Pancras, just two and a half hours away, and Manchester about three quarters of an hour away.

The Midland Railway was originally incorporated on 10 May 1844 into an amalgamation with the North Midland, Midland Counties and Birmingham and Derby Junction Railways. This became one of the most influential groupings, with access to many parts of Britain through joint lines and working arrangements.

The locomotives and rolling stock of the Midland Railway were the envy of all, with such masters of engineering as Matthew Kirtley and the inspired Samuel Waite Johnson adding flair and stateliness to their designs.

The Midland Railway also led the way in improving standards of travel, which other companies were forced to follow. They became a true leading light, second only to the Great Western Railway in terms of route mileage.

Its most memorable constructions, apart from the acclaimed station at St Pancras, are the viaducts and tunnels, which carried the line through the picturesque valleys of the Peak District. The line carried both freight and passenger traffic. Coal was unloaded at Bakewell Station and delivered to remote areas, while milk churns from surrounding farms were sent south to London, as was lime from Miller's Dale.

Julia at Darley Dale Station on the Peak Rail heritage line.

The railway transformed places along the route, like Buxton and Matlock, from sleepy little settlements to bustling towns. But the nationalization of the railway network sounded the death knell and the line fell foul to Beeching's cuts and closed in 1968, despite local pressure to keep it open.

In order to prevent dereliction and put the line to a new use the Peak District National Park Authority spent twelve long years negotiating with British Rail to purchase it. Eventually a deal was struck and British Rail provided a £154,000 fund to help with repairs. Once this work was complete the old railway line breathed new life in the shape of the Monsal Trail providing access to walkers and cyclists.

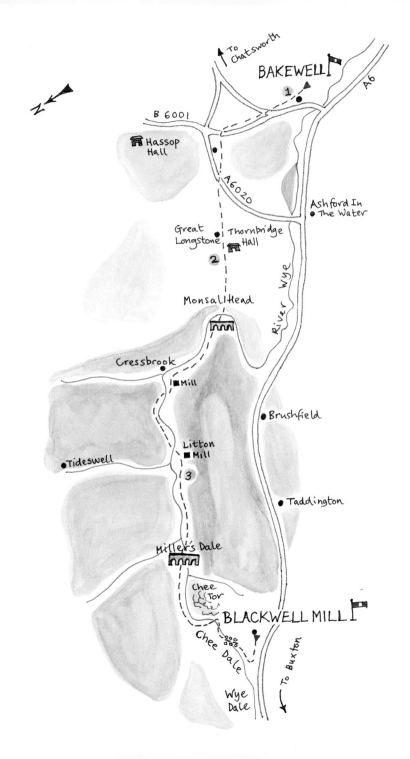

THE WALK

Bakewell to Blackwell Mill
8 miles / 12.8 kilometres

OVERVIEW

The route leaves Bakewell and heads north across rolling farmland that is dominated by the local estates of Hassop Hall and Chatsworth House. Turning west the railway line headed to the village of Great Longstone, once with its very own station, a facility shared with neighbouring Thornbridge Hall. The drama of the Wye Valley soon takes over. For the Midland Railway this meant building the glorious Monsal Viaduct. At Cressbrook village follow the riverside footpath for a while whilst the railway disappears deep under the Derbyshire hills. Rejoining the old line at Litton Mill continue on a straight run to the unusual double-viaduct at Miller's Dale. This is now limestone country where old quarries are obvious amongst the hills as the Wye Valley gets deeper and enters a gorge at Chee Dale. The end of the walk is simply stunning, a dramatic natural rock corridor to the junction where trains from London turned either to Buxton, or to Manchester. Today this might be a tranquil spot but this quiet rural ending once rumbled with the sound of locomotives.

STAGE 1

Bakewell to Thornbridge

Aerial view of Blackwell Mill, at the end of the walk.

Technically the official 'Monsal Trail' begins at Coombs Viaduct, one mile southeast of Bakewell. But for easy access and more convenient transport links Bakewell can offer an alternative start point.

Start to the east of Bakewell town centre, behind the old Bakewell Station, in a small industrial estate. Now converted into modern offices, the station is still instantly recognisable. Back in the late nineteenth century the arrival of the railway certainly didn't get a warm welcome from everyone. Both the Duke of Rutland and the Duke of Devonshire expressed early opposition to the idea of the line going through their estates. The Duke of Rutland eventually relented and the line was screened out of sight of Haddon Hall using a tunnel.

Heading northwest through the northern edge of Bakewell, past several industrial estates, the path straightens up and passes under a small bridge that helps you avoid the B6001 heading north towards Hassop. You will remain in this cutting for a short period.

Before the next tunnel Hassop Station is clearly visible on your right. Opened in 1862, it was actually built by the Duke of Devonshire of Chatsworth House, after he somewhat belatedly saw the benefits of the railway.

You head for a short time through a cutting before the landscape opens out for a longer, straighter stretch, crossing the B6020. To your right, the village of Great Longstone becomes visible. There's been a private estate outside the village since the early twelfth century and after the next road crossing you will see the grand perimeter walls of Thornbridge. In the past two hundred years it's passed through the hands of several entrepreneurs, many of whom have been keen to emulate the grandeur of the nearby ducal estates.

As you approach Great Longstone Station keep an eye out for the rather ornate building next door. This was the personal waiting room and station of one George Marples, a former owner of Thornbridge Hall and a man with aspirations.

After making a lot of money in steel and as a barrister, Marples moved to Derbyshire, to live the life of a country gentleman. He bought the house in 1876 and extended it to its near present form, adding lodges and cottages and

Great Longstone Station and the former private station of Thornbridge Hall.

landscaping the park. Perhaps his most lavish addition however, was the private station that he had built rather than walk the 500 yards from his grounds to the public station. He'd wait in his own private room and then get the train to move a few hundred yards down the track for him to get on. Today, Thornbridge Hall is a private family home and not open to the public.

STAGE 2

Thornbridge to Cressbook

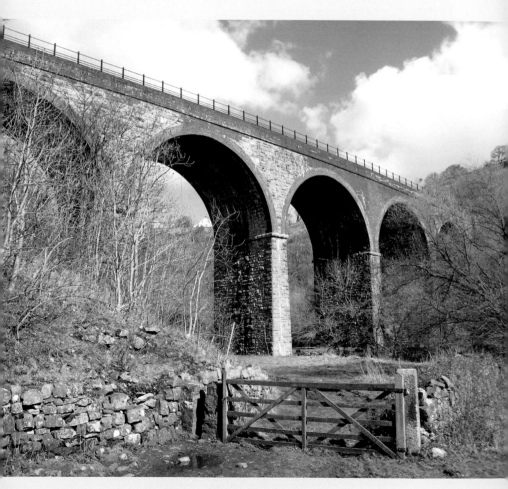

The Headstone Viaduct at Monsal Head.

Leaving Great Longstone and Thornbridge behind, the walk heads west entering a tree-lined cutting. This eventually opens out to give a pleasant view of the surrounding fields and hills of the Peaks.

The walk now begins to change in character as the gently rolling fields run out and the gritstone of Bakewell turns into classic Peak District limestone. For the railway engineers it was this change in landscape that posed one of their most serious engineering problems.

Unable to forge a straight route over the twisting valleys and rocky hills that lay ahead they had no other option but to go under them. The end result was the Headstone Tunnel, a massive 533 yards long excavation that was wide and tall enough for two express trains to hurtle past in each direction.

Today, the tunnel is closed to the public, the structures are not considered safe enough for walkers to explore alone. The Headstone Tunnel is a ghostly relic of one of the country's mainlines, a giant structure that symbolizes the Beeching era. (A project is however currently in place to open all six tunnels on this walk to the public once more.)

Instead of following the direct route as the trains did, a clearly signposted path takes you up and around to Monsal Head. The walk returns to the railway line at the Headstone Viaduct, the next impressive landmark.

A stunning 300 feet long, with five 50 feet span arches some 40 feet high at the centre, it's a structure that's become an icon of the nation's railway history. But when it was built in 1863 it was considered an eyesore and something that would ruin the dale. John Ruskin was a vociferous critic. He remarked: "There was a rocky valley between Buxton and Bakewell once upon a time, divine as the Vale of Tempe.

The locked tunnel near Cressbrook.

You enterprised a railroad through the valley – you blasted its rocks away, heaped thousands of tonnes of shale into its lovely stream. The valley is gone, and the gods with it; and now, every fool in Buxton can be in Bakewell in half an hour, and every fool in Bakewell at Buxton".

Standing on the viaduct today, surrounded by trees and with the burbling waters of the River Wye below, it's extraordinary to think this was the spot where trains from London would have burst out from the darkness, with passengers enjoying one of the most impressive stretches of line in the country.

The walk next enters a dramatic cutting carved into the jagged limestone. Up ahead another closed tunnel means the walk diverts down to the river. Here, you skirt around the limestone hill, which the railway tunnels through, taking you on a scenic journey along the banks of the Wye. It was the power of its water which fuelled the next major landmark of the walk.

From the flat-bottomed valley of Monsal Dale, the railway soon runs into one of the old industrial centres of the Peak. The imposing Cressbrook Mill was built in 1785, by the great industrialist, Sir Richard Arkwright. The original building was destroyed by fire but a replacement was soon opened. This became known as 'Old Mill'. In 1812 construction started on

The view up Water cum Jolly Dale.

the large Georgian building that can be seen today. 'Big Mill' used water from the River Wye to power its two large water wheels before steam turbines were introduced in 1890.

Back in the early nineteenth century the workforce consisted of a few adults and mostly pauper children, brought in on the railway from London and the south. Its manager, William Newton, was however known for his fair treatment of these apprentices, a far cry from some of the brutality experienced in other mills at this time. He provided them with reasonable standards of living and even built a village school. They lived in the cottages known as 'Apprentice Row', now Dale Terrace and slept four to a room. Manufacturing ceased in 1965 and this one time cotton mill has now been converted into plush apartments.

The path delivers you to the rear of the mill and the banks of the River Wye before continuing around the large basin at Cressbrook.

Cressbrook Basin

For me this was a walk that really sparked some fond memories. It would be fair to say that it was in this backdrop that my interest in the outdoors and in discovering what was out there in my own backyard first began.

I went to school not far from here and to be honest I didn't really like it all that much. So, to escape at the weekends my dad would bring me walking all around this countryside. Back then I didn't need a map because I had a dad.

I've still got a dad and so it seemed only right and proper to return to one of the spots he used to bring me to when we filmed this walk for the BBC television series. He also agreed to an 'on-screen' meeting, which was to provide one of those television moments that actually left me a little lost for words; a very rare thing indeed.

As with all my normal 'interviews' that are included in my TV walks everything was organized and in place. We met at the arranged spot in front of the lovely Cressbrook Basin, a broad expanse of water, accompanied by the sounds of bobbing mallards. The focus of this brief exchange was to explain to viewers some of my family history, how I first began coming to the area when I was about four. My dad went to lengths to explain that I was a rather 'independent' child and would usually be up above on the cliffs, rarely following him. He explained that the Peak District has a special kind of magic that makes people want to explore, which is why he brought me. It was all going well and exactly to plan.

But then came the trout-tickling story. Now, I have very fond memories of my dad taking me off and showing me how to do this. Not in the exact spot where we were filming I hasten to add

Julia walking around the bowl at Cressbrook.

because that's privately managed. So what I was expecting was for him to simply recount this jolly family outing.

But that's certainly not what happened. Instead he calmly took a moment, almost as though to recall the delicious episode and then wistfully said: "Touching your first trout gently under the gills is like touching your first woman – smooth, soft, sometimes slippery but very exciting".

There's not a lot a daughter can say to her dad when he delivers a line quite like that. It was a walk where I certainly learned a thing or two.

Follow the river upstream where the path hugs the steep side of the rock face very closely. As the path winds around two big bends it enters an altogether different landscape, a bit of a strange place, with an equally strange name – Water-cum-Jolly Dale. Keep your eyes fixed up to the left and you will able to see a bit of the old line as it exits one tunnel and then enters another. You can imagine as a passenger glimpsing for just a few seconds this tranquil hidden valley.

The path continues to wind through this beautiful, lush and silent river section. After the second of the two bends the riverside section of the walk comes to a close and you reach a second cotton mill at Litton.

This mill, established in 1782 by two local farmers, Ellis Needham and Thomas Frith, had an altogether different reputation than Cressbrook Mill, becoming notorious for its unsavoury employment practices with child workers undertaking fourteen hour shifts, six days a week.

It could be said the mill was doomed from the start. Needham, in particular, had sunk most of his assets into the venture. The valley was particularly isolated and transport for raw materials and finished goods were poor. By 1786 the barely profitable mill was put up for sale. There were no buyers and Needham and Frith struggled on. Needham's money had gone and he was farming on rented land, while Frith left the partnership in 1799. There was also a serious fire in 1811 and by 1815 Needham was bankrupt and had been given notice to quit. By 1828 he was a pauper.

It is believed that Charles Dickens based his character Oliver Twist on Robert Blincoe, a workhouse boy sent to this mill in 1802. He survived the appalling conditions and long hours, which included a paltry diet of porridge and black

Litton Mill.

bread for another fifteen years, before leaving to set up his own cotton spinning business.

In 1932 Blincoe was interviewed by the 'Employment of Children in Manufactories Committee', during which he gave a clear indictment against his treatment at Litton, stating he'd rather see his own child shipped to Australia than work in such a factory.

The mill was operated for a time by the Newtons of Cressbrook Mill but it was destroyed by another fire in 1874. Very little remains of the original mill, although there has been some impressive restoration and development in the area.

Both Litton and Cressbrook Mills owe their existence to the once thriving cotton industry. But today, they are quiet pin-up villages. And of course in those two hundred years that have passed in between, the railways have also been and gone. With no trains, no cotton mills and a large number of second homes the Wye Valley is an altogether more peaceful place today than it has been for centuries.

STAGE 3

Miller's Dale to Blackwell Mill

The viaduct at the start of Chee Dale.

The walk continues past the mill and the converted flats and cottages. Take the turning on the left, which crosses a bridge and then follows a steep winding path upwards until it rejoins the railway line. After following a tree-lined section keep your eyes peeled for examples of commercial lime Kilns, built in the nineteenth and twentieth centuries. Limestone transported from the quarries that opened adjacent to the railway and coal brought in by train, was burnt to produce the quicklime. This in turn was taken out on the railway.

The next unmistakable landmark is the Miller's Dale Viaduct, actually two viaducts standing side by side. Originally there was only one but by the early 1900s the line was getting so busy that to increase capacity a second viaduct was built to allow freight trains to pass express trains. Ironically it's the older of the two viaducts that today is in by far the best condition.

The viaducts lead to Miller's Dale station, an important junction where passengers for Buxton joined or left the trains between London and Manchester. With five platforms it was the largest station on the line. Unusually Miller's Dale was one of the few stations in England to have a post office on the platform.

Leaving Miller's Dale you begin the final part of the walk. The hill of Chee Tor, with its locked tunnel, forces you off the track for the last time. The descent down to the narrow gorge of Chee Dale and under a viaduct is dramatic. The stone steps take you all the way down to the riverside providing a great view of the huge viaduct above. Chee Dale is, in my opinion, one of the very best walking spots in Derbyshire, a picturesque river walk through a classic valley that culminates in a full-blown gorge.

Following the river westwards the scenery is packed with dense vegetation, steep stone faces and a beautiful flowing river. The path eventually bends round and you cross a long line of stepping stones. It then climbs back towards the former train line. Follow it upwards until it spits you out at the other end of Chee Tor Tunnel.

Straight ahead is another tunnel, this time open. After this limestone cliffs rise magnificently around you until you reach a split in the path. The line to the left would have gone to Buxton and the right fork to Manchester. Whilst these services are no more today, one line does remain in the area. It's a freight line serving the modern limestone quarries nearby. It still occupies the route of the Midland Railway from this point on and means that walkers never quite make it to the spa town of Buxton.

Head right and you arrive in the pretty hamlet of Blackwell Mill, the end the walk. This was a junction where trains once thundered all around. Today, it's an idyllic spot with a row of beautiful Peak District cottages, once the homes of a Midland Railway stationmaster and his three signalmen.

This short stretch of the Midland Railway covered by the Monsal Trail was the most ambitious and complex in the whole of the company's network. In the space of six miles it went through six tunnels and crossed the River Wye six times. Walking along the route today you can't help but admire the determination there must have been to add this route to the Midland Railway's portfolio and having built the thing, it's staggering to realise that after that effort it only actually had a hundred years use.

Cottages at Blackwell Mill.

Additional Info:

From Blackwell Mill you can continue along the riverbed under another viaduct until you reach the car park at Wye Dale adjoining the A6.

Bus services operate on the A6 stopping at Bakewell, Ashford in the Water, Blackwell Turn and Wye Dale.

Contact *www.derbybusinfo* for the latest timetables and services.

Recommended Maps: The Peak District, 24 OL.

gateway to the highlands

This walk will take you to the very heart of Scotland, into an area that has often been called the 'Gateway to the Highlands'. To the south lie the lowlands of Glasgow and Edinburgh, whereas to the north, it's a world of mountains and lochs. The route heads into the once turbulent world of the Highlands, a land of Scottish clans and the home of Rob Roy. But this fascinating walk will also reveal how the railway line helped bring civilisation to a region famed for its wild and violent history. Until 1800, few people chose to venture to these remote parts without good reason. This is a walk which promises to show how the railway helped this area turn from feared to fashionable in the space of sixty years.

Falls of Dochart, Killin.

history of the railway line

The Callander & Oban Railway Company was formed in 1864 with the objective of building a route through the Highlands, winding north, then west through Glen Ogle and Glen Dochart to reach the coastline at Oban. By this time Callander had already been reached by the Dunblane, Doune & Callander Railway built in 1858.

Work started on the new Callander & Oban line in 1866 and the single track passed Killin in 1870, reached Tyndrum in 1873 and Dalmally in 1877. Following completion in 1880, Oban developed as a fashionable resort, though economically the railway was never really profitable.

Other off shoot branchlines were added later. These included the Crieff line, which ran along Loch Earn and reached Balquhidder Junction on 1 May 1905. The five mile Killin branch opened on 13 March 1886, although unusually this branchline was privately owned and funded by local landowners.

The eastern section of the Callander & Oban Railway was scheduled for closure on 1 November 1965. However, the section between Callander and Crianlarich (along with the Killin branch) was closed following a landslide in Glen Ogle on 27 September 1965 and never reopened.

Today, the old lines have become a popular walking route and part of a massive cycle path running from Glasgow all the way to Inverness.

View over Loch Lubnaig.

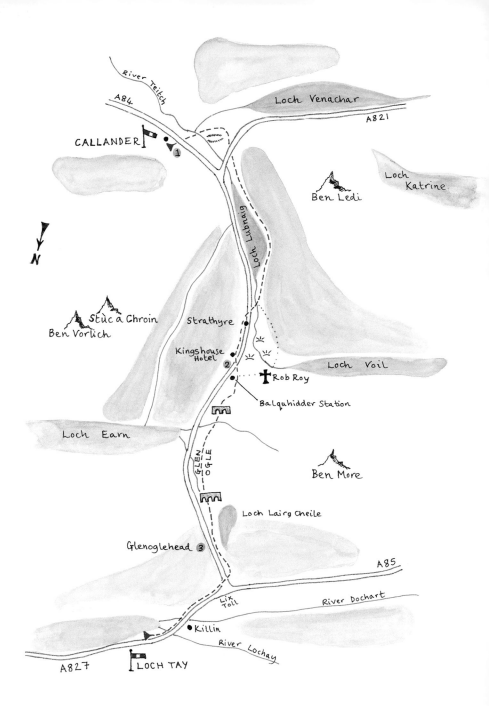

THE WALK
Callander to Loch Tay
23 miles / 37 kilometres

OVERVIEW

Most of this walk is a long steady climb up into the southern Highlands. It follows the river upstream from Callander along the western shore of Loch Lubnaig. North of the loch is the first village on the route. Strathyre was a holiday spot for Wordsworth, and sixty years later, the first station north of Callander. Long before that, this was the home turf of the Clan MacGregor and their most famous son, Rob Roy. As the railway approached Loch Earn the line split, with some trains forking right towards the water. The Callander & Oban Railway climbed upwards and headed straight through Glen Ogle. Three quarters of the way along you will reach the signature feature of this railway, the Glen Ogle Viaduct. Once you are over Glenoglehead you enter Glen Dochart. From here it's all downhill as you pick up the old Killin branchline. Victorian tourists would have once passed through Killin Village on the train to reach the pleasure steamer on the shores of Loch Tay.

STAGE 1

Callander to Strathyre

Aerial view of Loch Lubnaig.

Your starting point is Callander, a town that was carefully planned in the late 1770s around the main street and central square. But it was in the 1800s that Callander really began to gain attention. This was the era when Walter Scott, William Wordsworth, Queen Victoria, and of course the railway, came to the area. The wide streets of the 1770s certainly catered for the bustling crowds of visitors who arrived with the railway, all demanding food, hotels and carriages to take them on from the impressively large station.

Today there are few signs of the old station. Its former location is now a different kind of transport hub in the shape of a car park to the rear of the Dreadnought Hotel, off the main high street. Although there is not much to see here, take a stroll past the hotel and round the front take a glance up at the sculpture of a head. This was the head of a member of Clan McNeish, the dreaded enemy of Clan MacNab and an early sign as to the flavour of this walk.

The Dreadnought Hotel was built in the early 1800s by the Clan MacNab and owes its name to their distinctive battle cry of 'dread nought' (fear nothing). Whilst they were one of the local clans, their recognised home is at Killin, at the other end of this walk.

Cross the road and start to head out of Callander, just after some traffic lights the footpath slopes down off the road to the left. A railway signal reassuringly indicates you have now joined the old trackbed. The route very quickly takes you straight into the Scottish countryside, along a quiet wooded and tree-lined path. After a short while the scenery opens out and the flat floodplain of the river is all around you.

Roman ventures into Scotland were pretty fleeting, they

Remains of the railway bridge at the Falls of Leny.

had found the Caledonian tribes simply too ferocious. But the first landmark, the faint remains of a fort, is a reminder of one of those forays. You can see how the railway engineers built their embankment straight through the ancient site; so much for conservation.

A few miles to the west of you is Loch Katrine, a favourite spot of Scottish writer Walter Scott. There's still a steamer on the Loch named 'Lady of the Lake', after Scott's most famous epic poem. He was one of the very first to romanticise about these anarchic parts, but even he rather dramatically pointed out that this was where "beauty lies in the lap of terror".

For Scott and his friend William Wordsworth, the remote aspect and the unruly reputation of this landscape was actually of great appeal. Wordsworth first visited Loch Katrine in 1803, the first of three visits to Scotland which also inspired a number of poems including, *Stepping Westward* based on his forays along Loch Katrine and *The Solitary Reaper* prompted by a visit to Balquhidder. Their literary work, motivated by and even set in this region, (known today as The Trossachs), was like a nineteenth century PR campaign, drawing a new and rather up-market crowd to Scotland's mountains.

The route continues northwards passing the A821 before joining the riverside. A short stroll leads to the Falls of Leny, which in flood conditions can be a turbulent rapid of thunderous foaming whitewater. But you should also keep an eye out for the remnants of the old railway bridge just a little further upstream.

Continue along this pretty woodland walk until you emerge into an open patch of meadow. At this point it feels like you have reached a real milestone in the walk, it's here that you cross the divide between lowlands and highlands. This is the southern tip of your first Loch, Loch Lubnaig. At five kilometres long, it's certainly not the biggest you might encounter in Scotland, but tightly packed between the peaks of Ben Ledi (2,884 feet) and Ben Vorlich (3,076 feet), it lives up to its Gaelic name, meaning 'crooked'. The path continues its long straight progress north up the western bank of the loch. It then bends left, bringing the walk back in line with this 'crooked' loch.

Continue along the path northwards towards the end of the loch, crossing a footbridge over a small river. The footpath then temporarily leaves the old railway line (although it runs parallel to the old trackbed) and starts the long gentle curved approach into the village of Strathyre.

STAGE 2

Strathyre to Glenoglehead

The view towards Loch Voil and the Balquhidder Valley, from Balquhidder Station.

The valley bottom around the head of Loch Lubnaig, provides a small area of good farmland but otherwise it's a classic v-shaped glacial valley through which railway passengers travelled before entering their first Highland village.

Strathyre is where Wordsworth chose to stay with his sister Dorothy on 13 September 1803 after they walked in the local hills. You can only imagine what he would have made of this rather remote railway. Just like in Callander the old railway station of Strathyre is no more. It's been replaced by a housing estate, but in its day Strathyre did win the best kept station moniker.

Long before both Wordsworth and the railway, the Blaquhidder Valley was the firm territory of the Clan MacGregor. Over the centuries the MacGregors were in frequent conflict with the expansionist Campbells who very often had the ear of the monarch. Over the years, the MacGregors gradually lost title to their lands and became tenants of the more powerful Campbells. To survive, the MacGregors resorted to raids on neighbouring land, stealing cattle and anything else worth taking. It was this period of plundering and pillage that produced Clan MacGregor's most famous son, Rob Roy. Officially an outlaw, he has become a Scottish folk hero, given a distinct boost by Scott, Wordsworth, Daniel Defoe and even Hollywood.

Rob Roy

Often referred to as the Scottish Robin Hood, Rob Roy has become legendary throughout Scotland and the wider world as hero and outlaw. Born in Glengyle, at the head of Loch Katrine, he was baptized Robert Roy MacGregor on 7 March 1671, although as a boy he was also known as 'Red Robert' on account of his red hair. In later life Rob Roy became a well-known and respected cattleman. But when he borrowed money from the Duke of Montrose and then failed to pay him back the Duke put a price on his head and Rob Roy's infamous life on the run began.

Rob Roy waged a private feud against the duke until 1722, when he was forced to surrender and was imprisoned. Five years later he was released and pardoned. He died in his house at Inverlochlarig Beg, Balquhidder, on 28 December 1734.

Highland Cattle near Loch Lubnaig.

At this stage in the walk you have a couple of options. You can continue along the official cycle route which deviates west to Balquhidder and then rejoins the railway line south of Balquhidder Station, a detour from the line, but definitely one for those keen to visit Rob Roy's grave at the Parish Church.

Alternatively, if you want to stick as close to the old line as possible you can leave Strathyre and head north along the A84 (keeping the former trackbed to your left) until the Kingshouse Hotel where you'll pick up the cycle route again.

If you do have time to spare, the beauty of the Balquhidder route is that you get another slice of railway history because this is also the point where one railway became two. In 1905, The Callander & Oban line was joined by a branchline running west from Crieff, down the valley of Loch Earn to Balquhidder. If you choose this route you will still be on the National Cycle Route number seven. Of course, lots of railway lines have been turned into cycle track, but this one is pretty dramatic, extending between Glasgow and Inverness, a total distance of 214 miles, which sounds like some pretty exhausting pedalling to me.

From the village of Balquhidder the cycle path winds its way back towards the A84 and then heads towards the Kendrum Viaduct. This is a great example of the ancient meeting the modern. The bridge lay unused for some thirty five years until a missing arch was replaced in 2000 and the solid stone viaduct was given a sleek twenty first century look. It was the final piece on the puzzle and meant this section of the cycle route could finally be up and running.

Continue onwards and upwards until you walk under a small bridge and through some cycle bollards. The steep zigzag ascent back to the old Callander & Oban line then begins in earnest. As you climb up this path there will be a fantastic view of Loch Earn, as well as the two Munros of Stuc a Chroin and Ben Vorlich.

The view of Loch Earn from the National Cycle Route seven.

At the top of the zigzag you step back onto the Callander & Oban (you can clearly see the old line rejoining from behind you). Up here you're rewarded again with great views over Loch Earn and far below, the lower branchline that ran from Crieff along the length of the loch.

Heading away from Loch Earn marks the start of Glen Ogle, perhaps the defining feature of the Callander & Oban Railway. This was a long slog for the engines. A 1 in 50 gradient might not sound much, but this was considerably steeper than most mainlines would ever aim for. It was not uncommon to see two locomotives pulling or pushing trainloads along this stretch.

The steep and unstable sides of Glen Ogle were a constant problem for the managers of the railway. So too were harsh winters when trains occasionally got stuck in snowdrifts. Passengers were known to escape on foot, using the line of telegraph poles to guide them to safety. But this steep terrain ultimately proved too much for the line and on 27 September 1965, a devastating landslide occurred. You can still clearly see the spot on your left where the rocks spilled down the hillside. Dr Beeching had scheduled the line

Farmland along the old railway line north of Loch Lubnaig.

for closure in October. But with the landslide occurring just a few weeks prior to this it was shut early.

The day of the landslide was the autumn holiday in Glasgow and District. A British Rail 'Six Lochs Land Cruise' from Glasgow to Callander & Killin was planned and everyone knew it would be the last such excursion before the railway closed. But the excursion never took place. Instead, a sign went up reading "interruption to normal service". The landslide had been discovered in the early hours of the morning. Officially the damage was estimated at £30,000 and would take a month to repair. It never was.

From this entirely unplanned landmark you continue towards the railway's most famous intended landmark, the

Aerial view of Glen Ogle Viaduct.

glorious twelve arched granite Glen Ogle Viaduct. By the time the railway reached Glenoglehead the engines had climbed a whole 280 feet since the view over Loch Earn. You can imagine what a highlight this was for locals and tourists alike as they steamed out onto the viaduct. By this stage you are firmly amongst the Highlands.

It's also a good place to stop for a view over another defining feature of the valley. Long before either the road or the railway there was one major effort to bring civilization and communication to this part of the Highlands. Lying between the A85 and the old railway line is one of General Wade's military roads.

Built in 1749, it was part of a grand attempt to pacify the area after the Jacobite Rebellion of 1745. General Wade, Commander-in-Chief, is the man synonymous with these military roads, although this one below you was actually built by his successor, Major William Caulfield.

The view of Ben Vorlich from Glenoglehead.

After the viaduct the railway and road get closer and closer together and shortly you will be back down at the level of the road. Look to your right and there should be a stile leading to open ground. It's worth stepping off the line for a second here. This is the highest point you'll reach on your walk and it offers fantastic views back down the glen and across to the dominating peak of Ben Vorlich. You are now 700 feet above Callander, which shows just how effective the rail system was at dealing with the gradients.

In 1870, the Callander & Oban Railway ended right here at Glenoglehead. There simply wasn't the money to complete the line to the coast. But over the next ten years the railway was extended in stages, starting with the route west along Glen Dochart.

STAGE 3

Glenoglehead to Loch Tay

Aerial view of Glenoglehead.

Most walkers at this point would take the direct route along the new cycle track, which heads into Killin village. But you can still stick to the old line as it curves round to where Killin Junction used to be.

After Glenoglehead and the pretty little Lochan Lairig Cheile, the walk enters thicker woodland and leaves the comfort of the tarmac path. A long leftwards arc delivers you to what is left of the old station building and platforms of Killin Junction. Up until now, you've largely been walking along the old Callander & Oban Railway line, but the directors of the railway didn't fancy extending the line to Loch Tay. So it was left to the locals to build and manage their own branchline, which they did. Killin Junction was built exclusively as an exchange point for passengers and goods arriving on that new line. From here a small engine would have rattled for four miles down the slope to Killin.

The arrival of the Killin branchline in 1886 changed lives in this highland village overnight. The shores of Loch Tay could now be reached from London and the Victorians duly flocked, packing into specially chartered rail trips. But how many of those visitors would have stopped to thank the local people of Killin? They were the folk who had gathered together, planned and paid for this unique addition to the rail network.

The walk down to Killin heads through woodland and timber plantations, temporarily interrupted by the junction of Lix Toll and its garage where you will have to negotiate the road crossing of the A85 and A827. It then continues, running parallel and south of the main road before rejoining the main cycle route seven. You walk through a long stretch of woodland before arriving in the centre of Killin.

Standing amongst the unusually peaceful Falls of Dochart, Julia reaches the final stage of her railway walk between Callander and Killin.

There must have been a very different feel to this village before the inquisitive Victorians arrived. Before the tourists, the area was heavily influenced by the Breadalbanes Clan, part of Clan Campbell. For centuries the Breadalbanes had clashed with the MacNabs, and both clans once had castles facing each other across the shores of Loch Tay.

Killin remains the spiritual hometown of Clan MacNab and one of the few pieces of land the MacNabs still own is Inchbuie. This small island in the River Dochart, surrounded by the Falls of Dochart, is the traditional burial place of their clan chieftains.

Two adjacent rivers now stand between you and your final destination. The Dochart is crossed via the grand stone viaduct that overlooks the resting place of so many MacNabs. Then there's the River Lochay, crossed by a more modern, metal structure. Take a right immediately after this bridge and

The stone viaduct between Killin and Loch Tay.

then follow the path through farmland along the bank of the river. This leads to a glorious uninterrupted panorama down the entire length of Loch Tay.

This was the view that the Victorians flocked to, albeit by railway carriage rather than on foot. They would have been dropped off just to your left, yards away from a pier that no longer exists, to step onboard a steamer that again, no longer exists. But I think its fair to say that for those visitors, the gateway to the Highlands no longer held the fear it once did. The railway helped convince the population that Scott and Wordsworth were absolutely right. This is still an area of immense natural beauty and even the best efforts of Dr Beeching and landslides haven't affected that.

Additional Information:
A bus service operates between Callander and Killin.
For more information on times and fares contact, Kingshouse Travel of Balquhidder, Tel: 01877 384768.

Recommended Maps: The Trossachs, 365 OS Explorer Ben Lawes & Glen Lyon, 378 OS Explorer

Lambing season for the farms along the Mawddach Estuary.

memories of a golden age

North Wales tends to conjure up images of mountain scenery, rivers and lakes, which of course are all major tourist attractions. But this railway walk follows a line that was actually built to bring those tourists here in the first place. In the 1860s the race to control a route to the Welsh west coast began. This saw the English Great Western Railway build a line through Wales as far as Dolgellau, the walk's start point. But it was the much smaller Cambrian Railway company that built a line inland from the coast. Today this is one of the least visited parts of Snowdonia and it's this section, which allows walkers the chance to explore this very beautiful and remote area.

history of the railway line

This line originally ran from the West Midlands and stretched all the way to the Welsh west coast. It was one of numerous lines that ran across Wales by the end of the nineteenth century, connecting remote parts of rural Wales with the industrial heartlands of Birmingham and Manchester. The line was fully opened in 1869 and was popular with Victorian holiday makers, particularly those from northwest England, visiting the fashionable coastal resort of Barmouth. But it wasn't just

Looking back along the embankment on the approach to Arthog.

a line that served to transport tourists; it was also briefly used to carry slate. But like many local railway services in post war Britain, this line fell victim to the Beeching cuts in the 1960s. It was deemed to be unprofitable after the nationalization of the railways in 1947 and was closed in 1965.

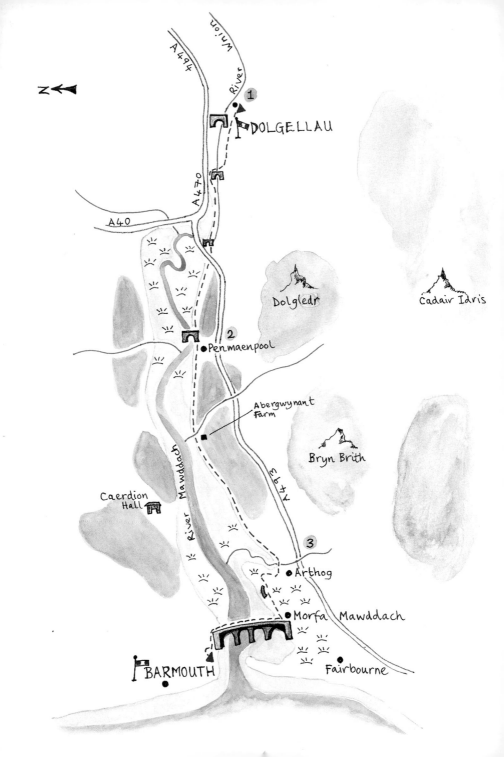

N

River Wnion

A494

1 DOLGELLAU

A470

A40

Dolgledr

Cadair Idris

2 Penmaenpool

River Mawddach

Abergwynant Farm

Bryn Brith

A493

Caerdion Hall

3

Arthog

Morfa Mawddach

BARMOUTH

Fairbourne

THE WALK
Dolgellau to Barmouth
9.5 miles / 15 kilometres

OVERVIEW

Out of Dolgellau you follow the river towards the head of the Mawddach Estuary. From here the old railway makes its own path across the reed bed and flood plains to meet the River Mawddach at Penmaenpool Bridge. Here the river opens out to look a lot more like an estuary. The railway path hugs the southern bank as it follows the corridor through the Welsh hills. Before you reach the estuary mouth you pass through the slate mining community of Arthog, where tramways once crossed the line taking slate down to the waterside. Finally you join a long curve to arrive at Barmouth Junction, the final landmark before the stunning approach to the town across Barmouth Bridge.

STAGE 1

Dolgellau

The River Wnion, looking back at Dolgellau.

The walk starts on the clearly marked cycle path by the river and road bridge in central Dolgellau. The other side of Bont Fawr (Big Bridge) is where the Dolgellau railway station once stood, but today sadly nothing remains. Modern transport rules and the cars and lorries of the Dolgellau bypass now rush by where the railway once stood.

From here you head across the open recreation ground with the town of Dolegellau on your left. After a short while cross the River Wnion via a footbridge and then take the left turn signposted for Barmouth.

It's here that you wave goodbye to Dolgellau proper, the old track becoming more visible. The rather noisy dual carriageway hugs the path to your right. But soon the clatter of the road is left behind. After half a mile you will be walking on familiar railway territory; an embankment.

Soon enough the railway line takes a more familiar shape as a long straight section stretching out in front of you, today framed by a beautiful avenue of trees. This stretch cuts through the silted up area of the upper Mawddach Estuary.

An extensive area of reed beds spans each side of the track, the largest in Wales. This designated Site of Special Scientific Interest (SSSI) is an important breeding ground for wetland birds and a diverse environment of salt marsh, swamp and perfectly flat grazing grounds. To the left rise the hills of Dolgledr.

Soon the gentle curve of this tree-lined trackway ends. A glance to your right across the estuary reveals the meeting of two rivers, the River Wnion with the River Mawddach, and from here you might just start to smell gold.

Julia walking through an avenue of trees.

The northern part of the Mawddach Estuary contains some of the most prized gold in the world. Carved out by a glacier during the last Ice Age, which ended about ten thousand years ago, the estuary is surrounded by high mountains, with Cader Idris (2,298 feet above sea level) to the south and the peaks of the Rhinogs rising dramatically to the north.

It was in the 1860s that the rush to penetrate these mountains began, when gold was found. In exactly the same decade the railway arrived. The area has produced rare finds indeed, making it some of the most highly valued gold and

Aerial view of the largest reed bed in Wales.

to this day, British royal weddings are usually topped off with a ring made of Welsh gold. Our current Queen Elizabeth II, the Queen Mother, Princess Margaret, Diana, Camilla and Charles all had wedding rings made from Welsh gold. The Queen was even presented with a kilogram of Welsh gold on her 60th birthday.

STAGE 2

Penmaenpool

Aerial view of Penmaenpool Toll Bridge.

Getting at the gold meant crossing the estuary and so the next major landmark of the walk comes into view. The trees become less dense and the landscape of reed beds once more surrounds you. After a short walk along a further tree-lined track the Penmaenpool Toll Bridge emerges, stretching out across the widening river.

This wooden bridge has served as a permanent crossing since 1879, connecting the railway station at Penmaenpool with the north side of the estuary and the goldmining industry.

But even before then this was far from a sleepy backwater and it wasn't just gold that stirred interest. There were natural riches of another kind here, with plentiful supplies of native oak, slate and wool. Back then the Mawddach wasn't simply a pretty waterway, it was the all-important transport link, which allowed industry and business to flourish in an otherwise remote rural location.

In the late 1700s the Mawddach was a busy shipping route with sailing boats plying the waters. Woollen 'webs' were collected and shipped across the Atlantic. This was a coarse flannel woven in the Dolgellau area, which slave owners in America used for soldiers' uniforms.

Boats coming upstream would bring coal from south Wales as well as lime and manure for the farms. Plentiful supplies of local timber meant that between 1770 and 1827 over one hundred boats were launched on the Mawddach, from the shipyards that lined its banks.

Eventually the bridge replaced the ferry service that ran here, providing one more obstacle to the shipping industry that was already being overrun by the railway.

You don't have to be an expert to notice the signs of a railway station at this point of the walk. Firstly, there's the signal box in the cream and brown colours of the Great Western Railway. Then there's the very familiar looking station building and an immaculately maintained signal. Penmaenpool is like a snapshot of the past, topped off by the centuries old George Hotel, built in 1650 that today provides an ideal spot for a quick drink and a bite to eat.

Leaving the pub and keeping it on your left hand side you pass the site of old sidings and a handful of buildings that served the station and the line. What follows on the path ahead shows just how much the arrival of the railway shaped this landscape. The walk leads through a tree-lined cutting, created when a finger of the hillside was blasted to create a flat and direct route for the train. Today it provides the perfect terrain for some easy strolling.

For over three quarters of a mile the embankment stretches out across the sands of the estuary. The valley may look wide and unthreatening but flash floods have been a feature here for centuries.

At the end of this long straight stomp you are rewarded with one of the great sights of the walk, the thin line of Barmouth Bridge, some four miles away, reflected in the water. As the estuary opens out in front of you Barmouth Bridge becomes a teasing goal for much of the rest of the walk regularly disappearing from view, then reappearing moments later as the railway hugs the line between the hillside and the estuary.

The walk continues along this track, pressed up against the estuary bank. From here on in the estuary serenely stretches out in front of you. After crossing a small metal bridge, with Abergwynant Farm to your left, the track curves round a small headland. At the top of this turn you can deviate from the track slightly for a well earned rest on the edge of the estuary. Here, a full view of Barmouth Bridge can be seen in all its glory extending, nearly half a mile long, between the northern and southern banks of the Mawddach.

Across the estuary, on the northern bank, Caerdeon Hall is also clearly visible. This was a favourite haunt of some

Penmaenpool Toll Bridge.

of the great writers of the Victorian era, from Tennyson to Wordsworth and Ruskin. The Mawddach has certainly not been short of its promoters in the past. The Great Western Railway advertised the trip to the Welsh coast as one of the "most enchanting in the world". It was Ruskin who once expressed the view that "the only walk better than the one from Barmouth to Dolgellau is the walk from Dolgellau to Barmouth".

Where the north side of the estuary was defined by its mining industry, the south side, which the railway line hugged, was more agricultural. Back on the path you can see there are still some beautiful old farm buildings. Look out for the remains of old telegraph poles which line the route here, bits of railway furniture, left over from the good old days.

It's all thanks to the railway that today walkers can now saunter through the estuary. Here you are afforded superb mountain views on all sides with little vegetation to obstruct the scene. It's almost hard to imagine this scene being anything other than a place of peace and tranquillity. But round the next headland there's a surprising discovery in store from an altogether different chapter in the history of the estuary.

STAGE 3

Arthog

Arthog village.

Amongst the trees you will discover some concrete blocks. Nothing to do with the railway, instead fast forward seventy years to World War Two. These were 'stop lines' or tank traps, west facing defences built to guard against a potential invasion launched via Ireland. Today this might well seem implausible but Ireland was officially neutral and active hostilities with Britain still simmered. An invasion was expected and given that the German forces held the bulk of coastal Europe the whole country was considered at risk of invasion and even the most remote beaches of north Aberdeen were defended.

During my own walk I had the pleasure of meeting Jackie O'Hanlon, who's a bit of a local expert when it comes to the trail. She runs a B&B business overlooking the estuary as well as leading walking and bike tours and of course all of them making use of Dolgellau's old railway line. But when she warned me to watch out for tank traps I realized there was more to this walk than meets the eye.

My walks have so often provided a unique opportunity to glimpse into the past and discover surprising pieces of history tucked away, so easily forgotten if it weren't for the opportunity to literally stumble upon them. On the face of it this quiet corner of Wales couldn't have seemed further away from the action of World War Two. But I was wrong. These 'stop lines' started as a series of concentric circles around London, but further afield as here, they formed barriers to potential approaches. The title is possibly misleading, these defences would not necessarily stop an onslaught but they were regarded as having the potential to slow it down and make it vulnerable to defensive fire.

Finding tank traps mid-walk was an intriguing step into an altogether different era to that of the Victorian hey day of the railway. I'm pretty certain they would have done a good job of delaying any sort of attack, sturdier in fact than even my Greek grandmother (sorry Yi)!

Some of the remains of 'Camp Iceland'.

The sleepy village of Arthog, clearly visible to your left, is a quiet collection of cottages, owing their existence to the slate mining in the area. Many of the slate heaps can still be seen on the hillsides, the last remnants of these once bustling quarries, which littered the slopes.

Arthog Bog stretches out between the village and the estuary and like the reed beds earlier form another SSSI, a habitat for many uncommon grasses and plants. It is also important for birds such as the Reed Bunting, Mallard and Curlew and is a good site for butterflies.

The River Arthog flows from above the village through a gorge, which descends in a waterfall. It's a landscape that also once offered another kind of rich pickings. In days gone by peat was dug up and taken away on sailing boats to be used as fuel. Today the area is protected by law.

Crossing a metal girder bridge you will soon see a small road and car park just off the main path and railway line, which is the site of the old Arthog Station. The station was primarily built for the local slate quarries and its workers. Slate was taken off to Barmouth and beyond from this terminus. The station was built very close to the water, on precariously low land that was prone to flooding. During one particularly high tide the stationmaster is believed to have clung on to his timber station in a desperate attempt to stop himself from being washed away.

The hillsides above Arthog are rich in historic remains, including burial chambers, standing stones and stone circles. The site was probably well used in prehistoric times because of its favourable location, close to the estuary for transport and with the protective mountains behind.

With the hills, quarries and cottages of Arthog to your left and the estuary to your right in a third of a mile it is time to leave the railway line for a short while. Take the tree-lined footpath on the right through the wooden gate and down to the estuary to discovery another hidden piece of history.

Keep following the wire fence all the way to the water and you'll start to see concrete foundations and remnants of old buildings scattered around. These are some of the remains of a marine training camp, known as 'Camp Iceland', reputedly used to prepare soldiers for the D-Day landings.

The presence of so much wartime activity here, in this sleepy, out of the way estuary might well come as a surprise for many walkers. But this tucked away military camp owes its existence to even earlier events. Back in 1894, a Cardiff entrepreneur by the name of Solomon Andrews had thought he could turn this waterside spot into a tourist destination to rival Barmouth. He came here with grand plans to develop villas and transport facilities. But problems with flooding and subsidence meant his dream barely got off the ground. What

Aerial view of Solomon Andrews' houses.

it did leave however was enough facilities for the marines to set up their training base.

Back on the walk you head through one more gate and meet a footpath that extends along the waterside towards Mawddach Crescent. The footpath eventually eases away left from the water's edge, leading you to a row of houses. These were part of the pre-existing infrastructure that the marines were able to utilize, all thanks to Andrews' failed holiday experiment. Today they are private residences.

The footpath now skirts around the rear of the houses, along a bend and through some thick woodland. After a short while you emerge onto a raised bed. You could easily be mistaken for thinking this is another railway feature but it is in fact leftover from an old tramway. It was built back in the 1860s to transport materials needed for the construction of Barmouth Bridge. A pre-existing feature that Solomon Andrews also made use of to transport building materials and visitors.

View back towards Barmouth Bridge.

One mile short of Barmouth and the old railway path meets with its modern day counterpart, the west coast line. In an area that lost so many of its major rail arteries to Dr Beeching's axe this section was fortunate to survive. Clearly visible ahead is its modern working station of Morfa Mawddach. The end of the raised tramway bed leads you into the car park.

This used to be the station known as Barmouth Junction and after Cardiff and Swansea it was one of the busiest rail terminals in Wales with the line from Dolgellau intersecting with lines from the Cambrian coast. Bordered by double track on all three sides and with five platforms, it was an important part of the railway network. The platform of the old station is still clearly visible to the side of the car park.

The tarmac footpath continues towards Barmouth Viaduct, along the rear of the Morfa Mawddach Station. To your right more tramways are visible but your attention is now on Barmouth and the bridge ahead. The wooden part of the bridge acts as the footpath and runs parallel to the tracks. The final stretch of the walk is fittingly shared with the quiet but definitely still active coastal line.

Opened in 1867, this viaduct, known simply as Barmouth Bridge, is the longest in Wales. Before the bridge, passengers were required to leave their train at Barmouth Ferry (on the site of today's Fairbourne Station) and complete their journey to Barmouth by boat. At low tides this involved walking over a 300 yard bar of rough gravel, which one contemporary commentator described quaintly as: "A mode of proceeding not very convenient for ladies and children".

The eventual construction of the bridge was one of the final and most complex pieces of the link, connecting England with the Welsh coast at Barmouth. At 2,292 feet long the bridge is made up of 113 timber spans and an 8 span iron section. Each iron column had to be sunk 120 feet below sea level through layers of silt and mud to find the rock floor. It was hi-tech too, featuring a sliding section at the northerly end that would allow ships to pass through.

Walk to the middle of the bridge and take in the stunning views back down the estuary along the old railway route, as well as out into the open sea. The original sliding metal gate mechanism wasn't a huge success, taking thirty seven minutes to open and close. As you walk to the Barmouth end of the bridge you can clearly see its replacement, a hundred year old conventional swing bridge (but even this has not swung open now for over twenty years).

So with your final destination ahead, this is it, the end of the line that once brought fashionable people from England all the way to the Welsh west coast. Here in one of the most 'Welsh' parts of Wales, where the national language is commonly spoken, you arrive at a town with the rather frightfully English name of Barmouth. It just goes to show that those Victorian railway tourists have certainly left their mark.

Julia walking over Barmouth Bridge.

Those visitors of the nineteenth century were just one of the many developments that this stretch of water has witnessed in recent centuries. Yet, despite the railways and the mining and the quarrying and the shipping and all the millions of visitors to Snowdonia, this walk still feels like one of the nation's better kept secrets.

Additional Information:
Barmouth is well served by bus connections via Harlech and Dolgellau and it is the area's only national network rail connected station. Details are available from the Tourist Information Office on 01341 280787 located at the railway station or consult the public transport journey planner: *http://cymru.trapezegroup.co.uk/ journeyplanner/enterJourneyPlan.do*

Recommended Maps: Porthmadog & Dollgellau, 124 OS Landranger

the whisky trail

This railway walk has a distinct flavour to it. Set along the banks of the River Spey, Scotland's second longest river and certainly one of its most famous, it's a route through the heart of a very Scottish industry. The Spey winds for a majestic 107 miles through northeast Scotland, passing the Cairngorms, before reaching the Moray Firth on the east coast. In between, its swirling waters certainly attract their fair share of interest. There are the salmon for a start. With enviable salmon runs and over eight thousand fish caught each year, it's one of Scotland's classic fishing rivers. But the waters of the Spey have another use; it's a river at the heart of one of the world's great drinks. This is whisky territory. And on this walk you can discover just how a scenic riverside railway helped transform a local industry into big business on a global scale.

Ballindalloch Castle.

history of the railway line

By the mid 1800s the River Spey already featured a number of distilleries along its course. But it was the arrival of the Strathspey Railway that made the real difference.

The line opened in July 1863 between Dufftown and Abernethy, (later known as Nethy Bridge). Three years later it was extended to meet up with the Inverness and Perth Junction Railway.

New distilleries soon opened up next door to the railway, which now offered great access to Glasgow and Edinburgh. But the arrival of the railway also inspired the founding of more distilleries and many had their own small tank engines, or 'puggies' as they were known, that most commonly ran on separate distillery lines.

In 1923 the Strathspey Railway became part of the London and North Eastern Railway (LNER) and through passenger services were advertised from Boat of Garten to the south via Aberdeen.

But like so many railways in the Beeching era it did not survive. The Strathspey line closed to passengers on 18 October 1965. Although the two stations at either end of the former line are open, serving two heritage lines, no part of the original Strathspey Railway has been preserved as a working track. Part of the line survives, the section between Craigellachie and Ballindalloch, which has now been converted into part of the long distance walking route, the Speyside Way.

Telford Bridge near the beginning of the walk.

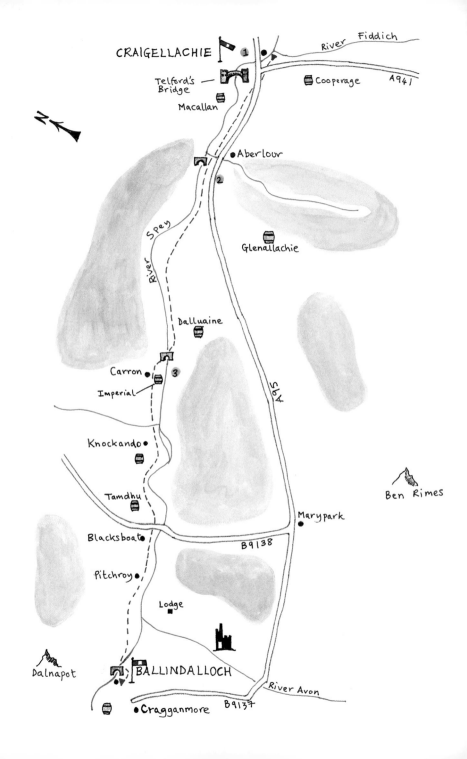

CRAIGELLACHIE

River Fiddich

1

Telford's
Bridge

Cooperage   A941

Macallan

Aberlour

2

River Spey

Glenallachie

Dalluaine

Carron

3

A95

Imperial

Knockando

Ben Rimes

Tamdhu

Marypark

Blacksboat

B9138

Pitchroy

Lodge

Dalnapot

BALLINDALLOCH

River Avon

Cragganmore   B9137

THE WALK
Craigellachie to Ballindalloch

12 miles / 19.3 kilometres

OVERVIEW

Starting from the remains of Craigellachie station you follow part of the Speyside Way, one of Scotland's great walking trails. From Craigellachie, the Strathspey Railway headed south, taking as straight a line as possible alongside the meandering River Spey. The only sizeable town en route is Aberlour, a name well known to whisky lovers. This railway walk then crosses open farmland and passes close to Daluaine, the oldest distillery on the route. After crossing the Spey you reach the village of Carron, once a bustling community beside the railway, but now a rather quiet spot sat beside the boarded-up buildings of the old Imperial Distillery. But whisky certainly hasn't gone away from these parts. Knockando and Tamdhu are both alive and well, despite the rather ghostly nature of their stations. The river and the railway both turn due south for a final long run. There's one more crossing of the Spey to reach the station of Ballindalloch.

STAGE 1

Craigellachie to Aberlour

Whisky barrels at Scotland's largest cooperage.

No visit to Craigellachie is complete without a visit to the bridge built by Thomas Telford. It was constructed over the course of two years between 1812 and 1814, long before anyone had ever dreamt of such a thing as a railway in these parts. In fact at this time Napoleon was still tearing up Europe and Beethoven was still composing. Looking down from above is like staring through a window into the transport history of this country. Materials for the cast iron bridge were brought in by river and canal; the great transport arteries of their day. But it was the arrival of the railway that helped a different industry to flourish here.

Since the arrival of the railway there's been no escaping the influence of whisky in the village. It has two distilleries, (Craigellachie and Macallan) and is home to Scotland's biggest cooperage. A staggering one hundred thousand oak barrels are processed here each year, most of them acquired second hand from the American bourbon industry.

Craigellachie is also where the two rivers most closely associated with the Scottish whisky industry meet – the Spey and the Fiddich, (which gives its name to the famous Scotch whisky, Glenfiddich).

Craigellachie dates back to at least 1750, when there was a ferry across the Spey to where the village now stands. Today it's a convenient stopping off point on the Speyside Way. This long distance path winds its way from Buckie, on the shores of the Moray Firth coast, southwestwards to Aviemore, on the edge of the Cairngorm Mountains, a total distance of 65 miles.

From the Telford Bridge head down to the southern bank of the Spey and follow the path as it hugs the first long

Aerial view of the snaking River Spey.

leftwards meander of the Spey. This snaking body of water runs for over one hundred miles from source to sea. It might well look like an idle waterway here, calmly meandering each corner, but its name originates from the Gaelic word *spe*, meaning spray or froth and the Spey is one of Scotland's fastest flowing rivers. In spate it has been know to rise over eight feet within a matter of hours.

But continuing into more tranquil territory the walk reaches the first great bend in the river and there's a rare tunnel, one of only four on the whole Great North of Scotland network. You can see the railway engineers had to work hard here in order to find room for the line between the river and the hill. The enormous wall to your left, holding back the hill, now acts as a support for the main road too.

After the complications of the bend, the old railway enters one of those familiar long straight sections and an avenue of trees that seems to go on and on. The undergrowth during the summer months is dense and in this enclosed world

Looking back at the Telford Bridge crossing the River Spey at the beginning of Julia's railway walk in whisky country.

there's just the odd surviving piece of railway history to keep you company. Look out for the milepost markers, which tell you how far you are from the local hub of Aberdeen, a fact probably more useful to train drivers than to walkers.

This long straight stroll brings you to the outskirts of Aberlour, a town that balances its whisky credentials with a quite different consumable product. This is the home of the renowned Walker family shortbread. It was here on the main street that Joseph Walker opened his local bakery. For well over a hundred years the business has kept baking and is now managed by a fourth generation of Walkers. One other thing has remained constant – it's the local residents who get to test any new biscuit products.

Aerial view of old Aberlour Station which is now the Speyside Way Visitor Centre.

The railway originally ran parallel to the river, which today means you approach the town centre via a long walk behind houses and gardens, with the Spey on your right.

You will eventually pass the old station on your left, complete with its original sign, now a visitor centre for the Speyside Way. But it's actually the building next door that's worth taking a closer look at – the pub in fact, but not just any pub though.

Today it's named The Mash Tun after the enormous vessel used to mix malted barley, water and yeast, the three key ingredients in whisky, which seems like a thoroughly suitable name for a Speyside inn. But it's a name with its own bit of intrigue. A pledge contained in the title deeds, made in 1963, states that if a train should ever pull up at Aberlour Station again then the name should revert to The Station Bar. It might be tempting to stray inside to sample the impressive

Victoria Bridge.

Glenfarclas whisky collection, one of only two in the world. But some of the more exclusive malts cost £200 a dram so it could prove an expensive stopping off point.

Continuing along the Speyside Way out of Aberlour you pass the Victoria Bridge on your right, known locally as the 'Penny Brig', the price once charged to cross the Spey at this point. Today this elegant suspension footbridge provides spectacular views of the valley. This at least won't empty your pockets, no charge involved for a Speyside panorama. But you don't actually cross this bridge. You actually leave Aberlour via the rather less stable suspension bridge, crossing the Burn of Aberlour, the chief source of water for the distillery. Water that makes it this far has escaped spending years ageing slowly in a sherry cask.

STAGE 2

Aberlour to Carron

Aerial view of Carron Bridge.

Continuing southwards the walk enters an area of farmland and forest surrounded by gently rolling terrain. You will pass through more open farmland, with expansive forests out to the right, before heading along a long, picturesque tree-lined path. This enters more beautiful woodland with the Spey in all its glory visible beneath the steep bank to your right. As the river returns from one of its lengthy meanders the walk passes the first distillery.

To your right you will soon see a large industrial area, something that resembles a huge chemistry experiment of intricate pipes and tanks. This treatment plant services the waste produce of the Daluaine distillery, which has been in operation since 1851.

When the railway arrived some twelve years later it slowly became apparent that the two industries could be of real benefit to each other. Eventually, Daluaine received its very own railway station – Daluaine Halt. As you continue on past the treatment works you will soon see that tiny station, its original sign still in place and its small platform visible in the undergrowth.

The arrival of the railway helped the Daluaine distillery go from strength to strength and the distillery expanded massively in the 1880s. There is quite a hill between the station and the distillery so the ingredients, barrels and whisky enjoyed their very own connecting railway known as a 'puggie line' after the little trains or 'puggies' that ran on them.

Distillery owner William Mackenzie first mooted the idea for this private distillery line in the early 1880s. But it took well over a decade before any tracks were laid. The final motivation was the opening of another distillery by Mackenzie's son. The

Aerial view of the Imperial Distillery.

branchline could now serve both sites. The only complication was that this new distillery was on the other side of the river. So the puggies joined the larger locomotives as both branch and mainline shared the track across the rather elegant Carron Bridge.

Before heading here you can take a small diversion up to the front gates of the still active Daluaine distillery. You can see where a small siding rail line would have emerged from under a bridge and come round into the distillery. Until the best efforts of Dr Beeching in the 1960s the puggies used to run all the way into the heart of the distillery. Today the work is done by a succession of lorries and tankers, a far cry from the days when Daluaine was home to several distillery owned locomotives, complete with their own livery.

After crossing the swirling waters of the Spey, Carron village and its station soon come into view. The station buildings, platform and level crossing gates are all still in

Imperial Cottages.

place. Even the station clock, now stopped, is still there. The distillery opened in 1897, Queen Victoria's Diamond Jubilee and was duly named Imperial. And to commemorate the historic event the company had a golden crown mounted on the highest malt barn kiln cowl. With the railway and the distillery at its heart Carron village once bustled with life.

But the distillery no longer looks like the thriving place of industry it once was. Imperial's problems were always its very large stills, meaning that it could not be operated very flexibly. It could either produce in large quantities or not at all and sadly it looks as though in future it will not be producing at all. Today only the buildings remain and Imperial has become a 'silent' distillery, a ghostly relic of an altogether different era.

STAGE 3

Carron to Ballindalloch

Overlooking the white water of the River Spey at Knockando.

After joining the tarmac for a short while you soon rejoin the old line along a tree-lined path with the Imperial distillery cottages to your right, built by the distiller for its workers. Locals' privileges also included use of a 'request halt', where they could literally thumb a lift and the train would stop and pick them up. Stroll along a Beeching railway and your thoughts are often focused on the past, on local stories and local people, a lost age still fondly remembered. But you can't forget that today the Spey still remains the focal point of a global industry and the neighbouring distilleries of Knockando and Tamdhu are very much a part of that.

The walk reaches them after following one of the Spey's long arcing meanders along a stretch of hedge and a tree-lined path. Despite the presence of big international business on Speyside the atmosphere around the distilleries seems amazingly relaxed and well, old fashioned.

A handful of multi national companies now dominate the Speyside whisky industry, producing household names like Johnnie Walker, J&B, Grant's and Bell's. Few distilleries in fact now remain in private hands. The Knockando distillery came after the railway and was built by John Thompson in 1898. Its name derives from the Scottish Gaelic meaning 'little black hill' after the village in which it stands.

By the time it was built it wasn't just the transport links which had made progress. Knockando was the first distillery in Scotland to be built with electric lighting. Whisky was becoming big business and today Knockando still shows off the old office of its Customs and Excise Officer, an important figure in any distillery, responsible for logging produce and checking that not too much of it had disappeared out the back door.

There's clearly still a reverence for the past at these modern factories. The walk continues to the next halt, at the distillery of Tamdhu, where the former platform, station

Ballindalloch Castle & some of the Aberdeen-Angus herd.

building and signal box can be easily spotted, preserved in all their former glory.

The path now heads due south into the estate of Ballindalloch Castle and the final leg of the walk. Unfortunately, the castle is firmly tucked away in woodland on the opposite side of the river. Since its construction in the sixteenth century the castle has been the permanent residence of the MacPherson-Grants. Today it's one of the longest standing private estates in Scotland.

With almost five hundred years of history and 23,000 acres to play with it's inevitable that the Ballindalloch estate and its castle should have had a significant influence on the area. George Macpherson-Grant in particular was clearly a forward thinker, being a key mover in starting up the nearby Cragganmore distillery. But the family was also the start of a very different kind of dynasty. This was where cattle from Aberdeen were brought together with cattle from Angus.

Julia in front of the old Blacksboat Station.

With plenty of spent grains from distilleries, the animals were always well fed. And today, a hundred and fifty years later, the herd is still in tact, the original Aberdeen-Angus family.

On your journey south, look out for the tiny, but lovingly restored station of Blacksboat. In just another five hundred metres you pass the rather grand Pitchroy Lodge on your right. This was the home of Captain W. E. Johns, author of the popular Biggles novels. He lived here between 1947 and 1953 and it's believed that at least fifteen Biggles books were written at Pitchroy and in the fisherman's hut by the river.

Keep following the former line over a wooden footbridge and through a small tunnel until you reach one more Spey crossing. This time it is a rather serious looking steel girder viaduct, still looking remarkably sturdy after one hundred and forty years. The bridge brings you straight into the world of Ballindalloch station, the last stop on your walk.

Ballindalloch was one of the busiest stations on Speyside

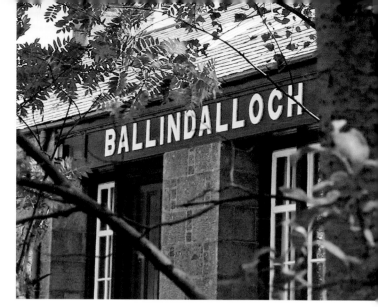

The old Ballindalloch Station sign.

carrying coal, malt, barley, even fish, as well as the weekly whisky deliveries on Tuesdays and Thursdays. But in the 1920s and 30s it also witnessed an altogether different surge of visitors. This rural station was transformed annually by the arrival of dressed-up partygoers all headed for the Granary Ball, held just next-door. Socialites from as far afield as Aberdeen would arrive in specially laid-on trains, intent on enjoying themselves and whisky would undoubtedly have been a key ingredient.

If there was ever a walk to build up a thirst then this has to be it. It's certainly a walk that's been carved by some key ingredients. The whisky relied on the Spey and its tributaries to make it what it is. The whisky and the railway relied on each other for business and it was the river that gave the railway a valley route through the Scottish hills and mountains. Today this winning combination also now means there's a perfectly laid out walk that allows you to enjoy all three. So perhaps the most fitting end to your journey is to head up the road to the Glenlivet distillery and sample a well-earned dram.

Julia crosses one of the many footbridges that cross the River Spey and its tributaries.

Additional Travel Info:

The Start: From Elgin there is a regular bus service to Craigellachie and Aberlour.

The End: Ballindalloch is 29 miles northeast of Aviemore and 14 miles northeast of Grantown on Spey on the A95. There is a local (infrequent) bus service linking Aviemore with Grantown on Spey and Ballindalloch

For more information see: *http://www.moray.gov.uk*

Recommended Maps: Buckie & Keith, 424 OS Explorer Grantown-on-Spey & Hills of Cromdale 419 OS Explorer

WEYMOUTH

harbouring history

Weymouth is arguably England's original seaside resort. It's where George III used to take his summer breaks, sparking a national obsession with the seaside holiday that's continued for over two hundred years. But sixty years after George III came here, so did the railway. The backstreets of Weymouth might seem like an unlikely spot to explore this railway history but there was once a line that ran south from Weymouth and across the unique coastal features of Chesil Beach and Portland. This walk is an ideal platform for delving into the fascinating stories surrounding the line and the surprising history of Portland harbour, as well as discovering more about this tied island's most famous export – Portland stone, which has quite literally carved the landscape you are about to step into.

View of Weymouth Bay from Weymouth Promenade.

Julia in Weymouth at the start of her walk.

history of the railway line

Since 1857 people had been able to reach Weymouth by train from London. But the railway line we're concerned with first took shape in 1865 when an extension line was built south from the town, across the causeway to Portland.

Today, the Rodwell Trail follows the first section of this old railway, which carried passengers and stone between Portland and Weymouth. The line was extended in 1878 into the Royal Navy dockyards and later in 1891 to serve Whitehead's torpedo factory at Ferrybridge. In 1902 the route was extended again, around the eastern cliffs of Portland to the village of Easton, creating the Easton and Church Hope Line.

The line was worked jointly by the London and South Western Railway and the Great Western Railway and was mixed gauge until its conversion in 1874 to standard gauge. By 1870, the first intermediate station at Rodwell was opened. The line continued to improve with the addition of

Weymouth Promenade.

new halts at Westham and Wyke Regis in 1909 and a new
stop at Sandsfoot Castle Halt in 1932.

But as with most of the other lines that we've been walking
on, the whole route fell victim to Dr Beeching. It closed to
passengers in 1952 and goods in 1965 and Portland once
more became a railway free zone.

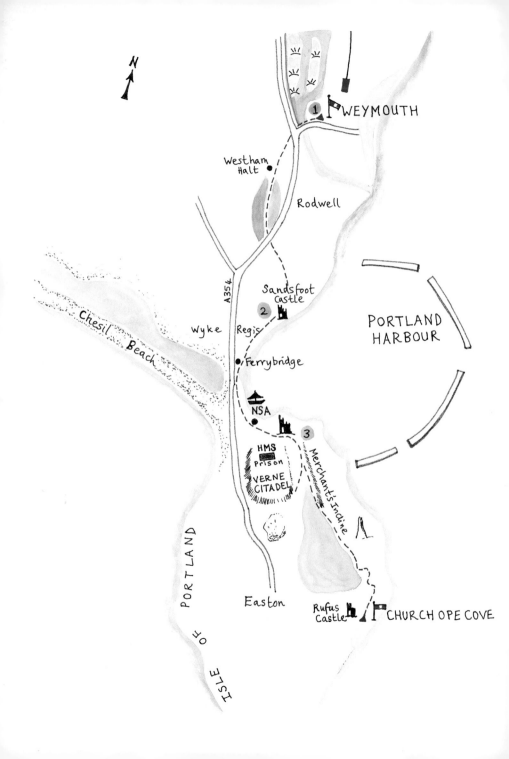

N

WEYMOUTH

①

Westham
Halt

Rodwell

A354

Sandsfoot
Castle

②

Wyke   Regis

Chesil
Beach

Ferrybridge

NSA

③

PORTLAND
HARBOUR

HMS
Prison

VERNE
CITADEL

Merchants Incline

ISLE   OF   PORTLAND

Easton

Rufus
Castle

CHURCH OPE COVE

THE WALK

Weymouth to Church Ope Cove

7 miles / 11.2 kilometres

OVERVIEW

From Weymouth Station the route heads south through a truly urban section of railway walk. The Weymouth & Portland Railway cut a clear path on an embankment, which today passes through backstreets and terraced housing on its way to meet Portland Harbour. Then there's a good two and a half miles of coastal views as the railway path hugs the harbour. You will take a direct route along to the end of Chesil Beach, the famous shingle bank that permanently connects the Isle of Portland with the mainland. This is where the Easton & Church Hope Railway once took over; building a line around the eastern fringes of Portland, through what would become Portland's naval base. Today, redevelopment forces you off the next section of the old railway line. So instead of following Portland's eastern shores you head onto its central plateau via the tramways which served the quarries. You then reconnect with the old track, which made use of the flat coastal plateau that overlooks the sea and Dorset's Jurassic coastline. You will follow the railway almost to its conclusion before stepping off down to Portland's one and only beach at Church Ope Cove.

STAGE 1

Weymouth to Sandsfoot Castle

Westham Halt on the Rodwell Trail

The walk actually starts where the old Weymouth Station used to be. This is now the car park of the RSPB reserve in central Weymouth, just off the Kings Roundabout and by the modern railway station.

Head to the southerly point of the car park and turn left under the road bridge following the water round until you see the bridge at Westham Road and the scores of yachts and boats behind it. Turn right across the bridge and then right again until you see the underground footpath, which takes you under and across the busy Westham Roundabout. The footpath then spits you out onto Abbotsbury Road and only a short way along are the large stone pillars signifying the start of the Rodwell Trail.

The Rodwell Trail might well seem like a purpose built by-pass for Weymouth walkers and cyclists, but it doesn't take long for its true origins to show through. The walk is barely underway and you arrive at your first station, Westham Halt, still sporting its station sign.

The trail sticks strictly to the path of the old railway line and so provides an ideal way to get across town and escape the cars. The only exception is at a dismantled bridge across Newstead Road, which forces you back down to the road. Cross safely and head straight back up the steepish path back onto the line.

Almost immediately you come to a rather more curious landmark on this railway walk. On your right you will find the site of a World War Two anti-aircraft gun emplacement, positioned to protect the area during the black days of the blitz. During the war years there was an expansive naval base down in Portland, a natural target for German aircraft.

The embankment, which provides so many views across the city, soon gives way to a cutting and a tunnel before the next halt on the line at Rodwell. This station is beautifully secluded and you wouldn't know that the suburbs of Weymouth were all around you.

The Rodwell Trail passes through the backstreets of Weymouth.

The stations come thick and fast on this section of your walk. Continuing down a stunning secluded tree-lined cutting and under the Buxton Road Bridge you reach the next station. When the line first opened, it ran without stopping right to the northern tip of Portland but as industry and workforces grew, more and more passenger stops were added.

Sandsfoot Halt opened in 1932. It was the last station to be added to the line, a simple single platform made entirely of wood. But it only lasted thirty three years before the whole line closed for good. If you have a careful rummage in the undergrowth on the left, you will be able to find the platform.

At this point in the walk it's well worth taking a brief diversion. Take the next left, towards the road and the sea and then another left. This is where the old railway line catches up with the coastline, which means your first sweeping view right across Portland Harbour.

With protection from the mainland, Chesil Beach and the Isle of Portland, the harbour is a vast natural bay and an ideal

Sandsfoot Castle.

anchorage point. No surprise then that Henry VIII chose to build two of his famous coastal defences here, one across the bay, at Portland and one right here; Sandsfoot Castle. It was built in 1539, and had two storeys, an emplacement for heavy canon, as well as living quarters for about fifty men. It was protected by a ditch and earth rampart, the remains of which can be found in some of today's garden landscaping. However, it was in the Victorian age, whilst the railway was being built, that the harbour saw its greatest period of development.

Construction of this modern harbour began in 1849 when the Royal Navy created a breakwater to the south of the anchorage, from blocks carved from local quarries on the Isle of Portland. This was completed in 1872 and created a much larger harbour providing protection from southeasterly winds. This series of stone breakwaters still protects the bay, creating one of the world's largest manmade harbours.

STAGE 2

Sandsfoot to Merchant's Incline

Julia at the top of The Merchant's Incline, Portland, overlooking
Chesil Beach and Weymouth Harbour.

Once you've taken in the views head back the way you came and onto the old line. Soon enough Wyke Regis Station comes into view, located in a deep cutting 500 yards long.

It's best to take the path left that climbs out of the cutting on its shore side, offering you a stunning panorama over the harbour. Beneath the waves that crash into the breakwater lies one far less obvious harbour landmark, the wreck of HMS Hood, a battleship that was deliberately sunk in 1914 to blockade the harbour's southern entrance.

When you begin to think about places of key naval significance on the south coast, it always seems to be Portsmouth and Plymouth that spring to mind, but Portland has been of strategic and technological significance for centuries. This next stage of the walk is about to reveal another surprising contribution.

Back on to the track itself, the cutting is now over and there's a new housing estate to your right, while the harbour stretches out gloriously to your left. This housing estate, however, should not be discounted. It was one of the key industrial sites along the railway line and one that had an impact around the world. This was the home of the torpedo, where Robert Whitehead, the inventor of the infamous self-propelled, cigar-shaped missile, built his factory in 1891.

This Lancastrian born engineer was the pioneer of explosives that could be detonated both remotely and underwater. His factory, which Wyke Regis Station conveniently served, covered 8 acres and had its own pier stretching out into the harbour, where testing took place. On your right, in the aptly named Whitehead Drive, you will find the very last remaining piece of the factory (to the far side by the modern traffic bollard). This memorial stone also signifies that you are now at the southernmost tip of the Dorset mainland.

Route of the dismantled railway along Chesil Beach. Portland in the background.

At Ferrybridge our walk leaves the Rodwell Trail behind and follows the pavement across Ferry Bridge to rejoin a footpath following the old line of the railway across a narrow spit. This distinctive feature was slowly formed as more and more silt, mud and shingle was deposited by the movement of the sea's currents, which eventually connected the Isle of Portland to the mainland.

In the background is Chesil Beach, stretching out with its salty lagoon known as The Fleet. This was where Barnes Wallis' revolutionary bouncing bomb was tested during World War Two. A strange contrast to The Fleet's status today as a protected, unique habitat for wading birds.

Back in the heyday of the railway this was also one of the most unique strips of line in the UK. You can imagine the trains, both in wartime and peacetime, busily travelling back and forth, the whole panorama of Weymouth and Portland in front of them. But it is as you get closer to the end that you finally appreciate the steep north face of Portland, which local author Thomas Hardy called "The Gibraltar of Wessex".

The Portland end of the beach is also one of the most vibrant spots anywhere on the south coast. Forty years after the railway tracks were ripped up this area is now occupied by the National Sailing Academy, host of the 2012 Olympic Regatta. The walk now follows a permissive path through Osprey Quay and past the sailing academy to Portland Castle.

The railway originally continued along the east coast of Portland, but today part of this route is now private land. So this is where our walk takes a slight diversion and follows its second former transport link, in the footsteps of the quarrymen and their wagons on the original horse-drawn Merchant's tramway. Today, it conveniently allows us to forge a route onto Portland proper, by walking up into the centre of the island.

From Portland Castle join the main Castletown road and turn left. Across the roundabout and tucked between two large blocks of flats is a footpath, rising steeply straight ahead. This is The Merchant's Incline, built to transport stone not passengers. The weight of the laden trucks descending pulled the empty ones up, while teams of horses transported the stone at either end. It was a route which successfully linked the piers and jetties at the water's edge with the quarries in the centre of the island.

Stepping onto this section is about stepping into another fascinating era of railway history. Work began on The Merchant's Incline in August 1826, making it one of the earliest public railways in the world and certainly the first line in Dorset. The climb up the tramway feels like the start of a new chapter. The urban backstreets are gone, so too the vast history of the harbour. Now the walk is all about this very unusual tied island.

STAGE 3

Verne Citadel to Church Ope Cove

View of the mainland from the highest point in Portland.

As you reach the top of the incline take a breather and look back over where you have just walked – Chesil Beach, the harbour and all the way back to Weymouth. The tramway soon splits, but make sure you keep to the lower line. This will wind round on a big arc, with the village of Fortuneswell down to your right. Look out for the old stone sleepers and even a horse trough carved out of a huge block of stone. The massive Verne Citadel walls will also be right ahead, a building so secure, it now serves as a prison. This imposing structure was built in the 1840s by convict labour and then extended in the 1860s as a massive military fortress.

To get to the quarries at the very top of the island a second major incline system had to be built. Our walk snakes round the front of the citadel, past some houses and then leads onto the incline and up under three bridges. It's certainly been left surprisingly untouched, with sections of the old stone trackbed clearly visible in places.

As you reach the top follow the tramway round to your left and an opening should be visible that takes you down to a still-active quarry. This allows a brief peek into this very historic industry that has shaped so much of Portland.

Portland stone, formed millions of years ago during the Jurassic Age, is considered extremely valuable. Not only is it incredibly strong, it's also quite malleable and easy to cut, making it a much sought after material in the upkeep and building of prestigious buildings. During the fourteenth and fifteenth centuries these quarries supplied stone for many major projects like Exeter Cathedral, Westminster Palace, the first stone version of London Bridge, Buckingham Palace and St Paul's Cathedral.

Back on the walk return the way you came, taking time to explore the area and the old gun batteries that are dotted around. The High Angle Battery is where shells would have

Active limestone quarries near the Verne Citadel.

been lobbed up and over onto the deck of any vessel that threatened the fleet moored inside the harbour.

Turn right onto the main path and then head onto the footpath, which leads down the east coastal path. Here, you can take in spectacular views of the Jurassic Coast. You can also see that you are about to be re-united with the original railway line, clearly winding along the coast down below you.

Joining this section, which was called the Easton & Church Hope Line, involves some rapid descent. It takes you past an intriguing local feature known as Nicodemus Knob, an artificial limestone stack that quarry workers left behind, proving just how much of Portland has been dug up and moved elsewhere.

Carry on past this strange rock pillar, past an old steam shed and along the side of the young offenders' institution, with the sea to your left. Then take the zigzag path on the left, which winds downwards and finally back onto the railway track. When you look back you can really see how far Portland's cliffs have retreated due to all the quarrying.

For a place that has been so utterly carved out by man the east coast of Portland is a surprisingly beautiful place.

Nicodemus Knob on the east coast of Portland.

Carry on along the scenic coastal path until you reach a fork in the track. The uphill slope to your right is a cutting that has been filled in. This used to be one of the most beautiful and dramatic parts of the railway, complete with a bridge that ran over the top. About forty years ago a Portland stone company came along, bought up this stretch of land and essentially filled it in, so they could get their lorries up and down. This is where you are going to part company with the railway track again and head left and round to a secluded cove.

When it was in operation, the Easton & Church Hope Line curved inland to its terminus at Easton, but this walk ends a short distance from the line at Church Ope Bay, one of the few places on Portland that has remained untouched by the continuous production of stone.

The path continues along and up past the tiny Rufus Castle, probably built for William II (called Rufus because of his red hair). It's likely that the structure we see today was the keep of a larger castle. Little remains of that first castle, with the possible exception of the arch that spans the path from

Julia at Church Ope Cove, the end of her walk.

Church Ope Road. The viewing area by the castle is a lovely place to look out over the sea. All there's left to do now is head down the steps leading to Church Ope Cove to finish the walk.

Believe it or not, the cove is the only place on Portland where walkers can get right down to the shoreline. Gaggles of visitors used to flock here in their bathing costumes to take advantage of the island's one and only beach. The folk of 1920s and 30s Britain seemed unfazed that they were just yards from quarries, naval ships and torpedoes. There was even a paddle steamer that would haul itself far enough up onto the rocks and shingle for visitors to walk a short plank onto the beach.

So the walk has ended, as it began, at a spot favoured by holidaymakers. But along the way all the flavours have been different. There's been military history in the shape of developments and defence and a huge protecting harbour, as well as the major excavations of the Portland stone quarries. The surprising discovery is that they were all served by the railway line, proving that Weymouth is certainly more than just a holiday destination fit for a king.

The Lulworth Coast seen from Portland.

Additional Information:

Start: Weymouth train station provides easy access to the start of the walk. Mainline rail services run from London Waterloo, Woking, Basingstoke, Winchester, Southampton and Brockenhurst to Weymouth operated by South West Trains.

End: A bus service is available throughout Weymouth and Portland. For bus services check: *www.travelinesw.com*

Recommended Maps: Purbeck & South Dorset, 15 OL

INDEX

Railway Walks with Julia Bradbury
AB2001 Blu-ray £14.99 (was £19.99)   Save
AV9677 DVD £9.99 (was £14.99)   £5.00

The complete television series, presented by
Julia Bradbury, as broadcast on BBC Four
and BBC Two, featuring all six episodes.

Also available on DVD:

AV9620
Wainwright Walks
Series One
£14.99

AV9641
Wainwright Walks
Series Two
£14.99

AV9917
Wainwright Walks
Series One and Two
£24.99

AV9676
Wainwright Walks
Coast to Coast £14.99

AV9590
Wainwright Walks
Complete Collection
£49.99

AV9762
South Africa Walks
with Julia Bradbury
£14.99

Order now from www.acornmediauk.com or telephone
the UK customer orderline on 0845 123 2312.
Don't forget to use promotional code RWFL for £5 off Railway Walks.